The Home Electronics Survival Guide

VOLUME 1

The simple guide to understanding, hooking up,
and buying **TVs, HDTVs, DVDs, DVRs,**
Home Theater, Remote Controls and more.

Written and Illustrated by Barb Gonzalez

ISBN: 0-9764894-0-6
LCCN: 2005910070

COVER DESIGN: Peri Poloni
Copy Editing: M.A. Giorgio
Cover & Interior Illustrations: Barbara Gonzalez

Warning-Disclaimer

This book is written to provide the most current, correct, and simply expressed information regarding home entertainment audio and video. Although, care has been taken to check that the included information is accurate, because of the possibility of changing technologies and human error, the author and Home Electronics Survival is not responsible for any errors or omissions or the results obtained from use of such information.

You are urged to read all available material and owner's manuals to assure that you are fully informed on the workings of your products. This guide should be used as a general guide and not the ultimate source of audio and video information. The purpose of this guide is to educate and entertain. The author and Home Electronics Survival shall not be liable or responsible to any person or entity with respect to any loss or damage caused or alleged to be caused, directly or indirectly by the information contained in this book. *If you do not wish to bound by the above, you may return this book to the place of purchase for a full refund.*

Trademark Notice

This book comments and describes various audio and video products. Many of these products are identified by their trade names. While care has been taken to include all trademark and registered trademarks, use of a term in this book should not be regarded as affecting the validity of any trademark or service mark. You should investigate a claimed trademark before using it for any purpose other than to refer to the product.

SEND US YOUR COMMENTS:
Let us know what you think or what you would like to see.
E-mail us at: info@home-electronics-survival.com.

HOW TO ORDER:
For single book orders, go to our website at www.home-electronics-survival.com.
For quantity orders or customized books contact us at: P.O. Box 1296, Cedar Ridge, CA 95924;
or email us at info@home-electronics-survival.com.

In memory of
Mario A. Gonzalez

This book is dedicated
to our son, Evan,
who has been patient as his
Mother wrote and illustrated
this book.

Acknowledgements

First and foremost I want to thank my family for their love and support while I pushed through the huge task of writing and drawing illustrations. My thanks and love to my son, Evan and to Wayne Jeffrey Cox who had to endure the stress of getting this book out. My ultimate gratitude to my mother, Fay Rosenstock, who came through for me when I needed it, and taught me to be resourceful. And to my father, Barre, for his love and support; and to my brother, Mike, who taught me to love electronics when he dragged me in to listen to reel-to-reel tapes and hi-fi stereo sound.

I also want to thank my co-workers at **the good guys** store in Studio City, California. My deepest appreciation goes to Tim Starks who shared a passion for video and constantly shared new technology. Without Tim, I would not have the depth of knowledge that I do. Also thanks to the other cronies who taught me, took care of me and kept me straight, Mike Wilson, Greg Imel my resource audio tweak, Jovan, and to the trainer who made it simple for me to learn technology, Manny. Also, with heartfelt love and thanks to Barry Mannheimer whose belief in me gave me the courage and belief that I could do anything including changing my life. And to Joe D'Amato whose understanding and support was so appreciated at a difficult time in my life. And to Paul Crevelli for the support and information he was always willing to share.

Special thanks to Dory Willer, who after 30 odd years, gave me a great gift of a push to get the book out, and resources to take me on my way. What an awesome coach she is. And to Eva Gregory who keeps me moving forward and in a prosperous state of mind.

And a huge thanks to the Consumer Electronics Association for their support. To Gary Shapiro, Matt Swanston and John Tunnell and the team who offered encouragement, knowledge and support along the way.

Preface

My years on the sales floor at an electronics retailer taught me that many people fear electronics. Just because you live in the world today and know what a DVD player is, doesn't mean you know how it works, how to set it up, how to use it. Mostly we all just fake a level of understanding; we don't ask questions because we think everyone else already knows it and we're the one left behind. You don't have to fake anything here. I know that people just turn on their TVs and hope for the best.

You may be getting by with your home entertainment. You call your son-in-law and ask questions when you need to learn something new, or you might call him again and again to remind you how you get rid of the green "3" constantly displayed on the TV screen. There's a benefit. When you buy new equipment, it does give you an opportunity to have them over for dinner and see your daughter. Or maybe you are a single woman (or even married) and you learned the damsel-in-distress-act works to get out of learning to do it yourself (and it makes your man feel important); but how do you feel when he's not around?

At some point, you and your TV will be left alone. You have equipment in your home that can give you news or entertainment. If you own the equipment it is certain that you will want to watch some show at some time. When that time comes, it will be you, the TV and the remote control (the stuff horror movies are made of).

It wasn't that long ago when watching TV meant hooking up rabbit ears or a rooftop antenna, pulling a button, and watching one of the 3 local TV stations. It has been barely 20 years since the introduction of Cable TV, and now they expect you to hook up 3 or more components, set up a home theater, and understand how to record without VHS tapes!

How can you expect to be anything BUT confused? When staring at 5 remote controls, buttons, menus, connections and cables, it is only natural to feel overwhelmed. I notice when I go into a store, or get a new remote control, that I have that same, 50-buttons-in-your-face panic. It's *because* I still allow myself to experience that feeking of overwhelm, that I can translate complex technology.

When I started writing this book, I planned to include it all. What I found was that, in this illustrated simple format, the book would have been 600 pages! Other guides to home theater come in at the same page count as this book, but they have *few pictures.* And the drawings they include are either for entertainment, schematics or technical charts. Therefore, I have split the book into volumes. This first volume covers general understanding, buying and hooking up your equipment. Other volumes in the series will be dedicated to setting up your equipment when you get it home and how to use all those features and remote controls, and to buying equipment.

Home entertainment is toys for adults. We have lost the fun in the complexity and frustration. My aim is to bring it back. My approach is to give short explanations accompanied by friendly and fun real life illustrations that you can relate to. We remember more when there's play involved. Although you can get an overall understanding by skimming through the book, you will probably want to clarify some of the information by reading the text. In the book, you will get the answer to many mysteries by telling you not only about the technology but about the history, politics, and economics that are behind why some products are designed as they are, and why HDTV is happening at all!

I've done my best to be simple and still a particular subject may just not make sense to you. If you find any part of this book confusing, feel free to e-mail us at info@home-electronics-survival.com. We'll be glad to help you out...

Table of Contents

Introduction

This book was not written for the home theater enthusiast. It was written for anyone who has a TV. It was also written for people purchasing new equipment who may understand how some features work but are *not quite sure why things work the way they do.*

From many years of experience with customers who were frustrated with their equipment, it became apparent that, when they understand why they have to do things a certain way, they can remember and reason how to do it. Why do you put your TV on Channel 3 or Input 1, and what does that mean, anyway? More than "put this here and put that there" instruction, the explanation of how things work and why, will expose the magic and finally make sense to you. When things make sense, we are comfortable. When we have nagging questions, we are uneasy.

Assumptions

The only assumption I make is that you own a TV and you have been frustrated by some aspect of buying, hooking up, or using it.

That's the big problem in life, and in technology in particular...we make assumptions about what others understand, expect, or we assume that they know what we know. After all, just because you've heard of an HDTV doesn't mean you understand the word "resolution". Just because a salesperson tells you a TV has a certain number of scan lines or a home theater receiver has "surround sound", and you've heard those terms, doesn't mean you know what they are. In fact, you may even be tripped up by the term "home theater receiver", as was the case in a recent conversation I had with a family member. **It will help if you first scan through the section entitled "Tower of Babble" to familiarize yourself with some terms frequently used in the book.**

Before you begin...

You may be skeptical that you could ever understand technology. You may say, "I don't get this stuff", or "I'm not good at figuring this out", or "I can't understand the directions and manuals" and you may have resigned yourself to "I don't care, anyway."

It's not that technology is all that difficult to understand, it's just that *it hasn't been explained to you in simple, everyday language.* But you'll have to overcome that disbelief that you can feel comfortable with technology first...

So, you'll have to change your attitude to start. While just being positive, having fun and exploring is the outlook you want, it may help to explore why we all don't take on understanding something new. There may be a *payoff* for you to need help with electronics. If you don't learn to do it, then *someone else has to do it for you.* If you never learned how to turn on the stove, someone would have to cook for you. If you don't learn to program the VCR (or DVR) you can ask someone else to do it. That's a nice payoff. But the *cost* is that you don't have the freedom to whip up a snack when others are gone--or, regarding home entertainment, you don't have the freedom to say, "hey, that would be fun to record" or even the freedom to watch a movie when your helper is not around.

Take back your freedom. Realize that you can take it slow and you will have a better understanding than you do now.

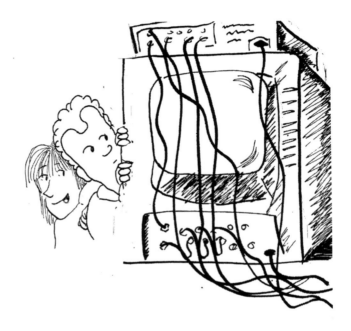

It's not that technology is hard to understand— it's just that it has never been explained to you in simple English.

What you'll learn

- Terms—so that you can follow this guide or an owner's manual.
- How the picture and sound get to your TV.
- Why you have a Cable TV box or Satellite receiver box and how you hook it up.
- The difference between today's NTSC TVs, ATSC digital, and HDTVs.
- How HDTVs work and how to choose an HDTV.
- What you'll need to receive HDTV.
- Identifying connections on your TV and components.
- What cables to use to get the best quality picture and sound.
- How to plan and hook up your equipment.
- Where to put your TV and how to place surround sound speakers in your room.
- How to go about buying new equipment.
- Buying considerations for TVs and most types of equipment out there today.
- Features you need and may want on your equipment.
- What you'll need to set up a home theater.

How to use this book.
Getting the most from this Guide...

Yes, this is a big book. I recognize that while many people want to get an understanding of technology, they don't care about all the details. Reading this book completely can give you a comprehensive lesson in home entertainment. However, it is designed so that you can skim through the pictures, illustration explanations and highlighted information and have an idea about how it all works. You can use the book as a reference for terms or as you need to hookup of buy new items. It will also be a good reference to re-hook up your existing items.

First, look over the "tower of babble". Even in the simplicity of this book, there will be some terms that you have heard and other terms that you say, "I've never heard it called that..." Familiarizing yourself with the terms, or referring back when you run across a term in a later chapter will help you learn more about the equipment.

After that, I recommend that you breeze through the book. If something is of interest to you, you can read in more detail. Reading through the GETTING THE PICTURE chapter will give you a good foundation for any discussion regarding your TV and your everyday watching habits.

Here's a breakdown of what you can get from each chapter:

GETTING THE PICTURE Chapter: You will learn the basics of how a picture reaches your TV. This will help you when you hook up your TV or home entertainment system. It will help you to understand why you turn on your TV to channel 3, and about inputs. This will give you an understanding of how to change inputs, how to program your recording device and more. Once you understand the concepts in this chapter, the rest will begin to make sense.

DIGITAL AND HIGH DEFINITION TV Chapter: In this chapter you will be able to find your way through the maze of what is happening with HDTV. Reading this chapter will allow you to understand many of the terms you will hear, not only as you go out to buy digital and HDTV, but also decipher what you may hear in the media. It will give you assurance in buying an HDTV today, and you will understand the reasons behind much of the confusion. Digital and HDTV is a subject with lots of new technology and is influenced by the needs of everyone from the movie studios to Politics protecting you from outdated technology. This chapter sheds light on all aspects of the digital TV revolution.

Ins and Outs of CONNECTIONS Chapter: In this chapter you will make sense of all those connections on your equipment. Unlike our man on the cover, the little terminals will not overwhelm you as you take it one step at a time to learn about inputs and outputs and how to recognize the different types available.

Untangling the Web of CABLES Chapter: Here you will learn about how cables transfer sound and picture and how the quality and types of cable will determine the quality of the picture and sound your receive. In the Cables chapter, you will begin to make your decision of how you want to hook up your equipment. You will get the information on which to make your choices.

HOOKUP PLANNING AND PREPARATION Chapter: This chapter shows you how to take the confusion out of hooking up your system. Here you will learn where you will place your TV and home theater and how the layout of your room will influence that decision. After reading this chapter you will be well on your way to hooking up your system on your own, in an organized, less stressful manner.

I recommend that **read through the glossary words at the beginning of the chapter**. As you come across the word, look it up in the glossary in the back of the book. This can help you decipher jargon you may be finding if you read owner's manuals, or while buying, hooking up or using your equipment.

You can also skim through the book reading the captions and call outs that look like this.

Later you can read more detail as you need...

However you choose to use this book, my sincere hope is that it will give you some comfort and confidence in hooking up and using your home entertainment equipment so that you will no longer feel intimidated by your TV and components. And once you've mastered one thing you never thought you could, what else could you do?

The "Tower of Babble"
Terms used in Home Entertainment

We experience it when we talk to a sales person. We see it online, in advertising, from friends. When new technology comes out, it is given a number of names. (Digital video recorders are a prime example, as they are called DVRs, PVRs, HDDs, Hard Disc Recorders, etc.) It's like the biblical Tower of Babel. Each group uses a different language and we all begin to have trouble understanding each other.

To turn this jargon into plain English, it is important to define some basic terms used in Home Entertainment. Familiarize yourself with these words to help you when reading further:

TV: To be absolutely clear, this refers to the television set.

AUDIO: This refers to sound.

VIDEO: This refers to picture only. (It can also be short for a VHS or other videotape player, camera or recorder.)

A/V: This is "audio/video" and is making reference to something that has both audio and video capabilities.

COMPONENT OR DEVICE: This is a piece of equipment, usually other than your TV (although some remotes refer to TVs as a device). Components include everything from VCRs to DVDs to DVRs to CD players, and sometimes refer to Cable TV or Satellite boxes.

SIGNAL: This is the electronic sound and/or picture information that is sent from a TV station to your home This audio and/or video information flows in and out of your components which ultimately you see on your TV and hear from speakers (either speakers on the TV or separate home theater speakers.)

The signal can come directly from a DVD player or other device that reads information from a disc, tape or other, and then be sent on to another piece of equipment including your TV or stereo. Cables carry signals, and signals can be sent wirelessly and picked up by an antenna or receiver. The quality of the signal is altered by the quality of the connections on the component and the quality of the cable. (For more about signals see Tuner Chapter 1.)

"JACKS" OR "TERMINALS" OR "PLUGS" OR "HOOKUPS": These are the actual connectors on the back of your equipment. They make up...

    INPUTS: The connection that brings the signal into a TV or component.

    OUTPUTS: The connection that sends the signal out from a component to be received by another component or a TV.

"DIRECT VIEW" or "CRT" or "PICTURE TUBE" or "TRADITIONAL TV": These terms refer to the type of TV that has been around since the beginning of TVs. They have picture tubes that display the TV's picture. (For how a CRT works, see Digital and High Definition chapter.)

HOME THEATER: In general this has come to refer to a system with a TV and a sound system that produces surround sound as it does in a movie theater. There are many ways to achieve the effect of surrounding us with sound. It does not refer only to those who have actual home theaters, that is a theater room in your home.

"A/V RECEIVER" or "HOME THEATER RECEIVER": At first receivers were for our stereo sound (and we called them "stereos"). We would hook up our phono, cassette decks, etc. The sound was amplified then played out of speakers. It was called a receiver because it received sound from outside sources (like your cassette deck) or from a radio tuner. Today most receivers also accept a video signal that is sent on to the TV (if you choose to hook it up that way). That is why it is referred to as an "A/V receiver"—it stands for "audio and video receiver." A "Home Theater Receiver" is an A/V receiver that also plays surround sound and may play digital surround sound like Dolby Digital® or DTS™. .

TUNER: Described in the first chapter, this is the device inside your TV, VCR, Satellite or Cable TV boxes, or set top box that changes the channel (tunes in to a frequency.)

SATELLITE RECEIVER or SATELLITE BOX: The piece of equipment that the Satellite signal comes into. It is the box that has a tuner to change Satellite channels and may be used to unscramble signals. Satellites send a digital signal and need to have the signal converted so it can play on your TV. These boxes do that (see Getting the Picture Chapter for a better understanding of Satellite receivers or boxes.)

CABLE TV: A source of TV programming that sends various stations through a cable into your home.

    BASIC CABLE: This is the line up of stations, usually including local TV stations, that come to you without a premium charge.

    PREMIUM STATIONS: Usually you are charged extra for certain movie stations and others that are not offered in the basic package. These signals are scrambled before you receive them so they require a Cable TV box or decoder of some sort in order to unscramble them for your TV. When you pay for the channel your box is sent information from the Cable TV company that allows the Cable TV box to unscramble them.

    DIGITAL CABLE TV: Here the information is sent to your home via cables that are capable of sending (transferring) a digital signal. It is explained in Getting the Picture chapter.

"BROADCAST TV" or "OFF-AIR TV" or "OTA" (or "OVER-THE-AIR ANTENNA"):
TV stations send their programming out over air wave frequencies that are received by an antenna. Often this is referred to as the signal from an antenna. It can be sent
        VHF: channels 2-13
or   UHF: channels above 13
Your TV will use its tuner to change from one channel to the next. Although TVs may pick up a signal without an antenna, you'll want an antenna to get a better picture.

"DVR", or "PVR", or "HDD", or "HARD DISC DRIVE", or "DIGITAL VIDEO RECORDER":
We've often heard of these devices by brand names like "TiVo"® or "RePlayTV®" but it is becoming common on digital cable and satellite receiver boxes. (And showing up integrated in TVs and other devices.) This product records shows to a hard disc drive like the hard disc that holds your information on the computer. (It can actually record whatever you hook into it, like a camcorder or other device.) We hear a lot about "pausing live TV". Along with recording shows that are stored on the hard disc, these devices will record whatever you are watching into a short term, temporary memory that you can then rewind or pause for a period of time. Usually changing channels will reset the temporary memory and, if you are to switch back, you won't be able to rewind the channel you were previously watching.

DIGITAL AND ANALOG SIGNALS: The digital world came about by a computer's ability to turn 1's and 0's into a variety of information, pictures and sound. Ultimately, any picture or sound must be converted to analog. Picture must be converted to lightwaves for us to see, and digital audio converted to soundwaves for us to hear. You can learn more about digital and analog in the Getting the Picture Chapter, and in the digital to analog section of the HDTV chapter.

Getting the Picture

WHAT YOU WILL LEARN IN CHAPTER 1...

-How the picture gets to your TV—what it means to change inputs.

-Why you sometimes have to push the TV/VCR button.

-Why you sometimes need to put your TV on channel 3

-Why you need a Cable TV box/Satellite receiver box.

-How you can watch more than one channel at a time.

-Why you need a separate Cable TV box/Satellite receiver for each TV and the exceptions to the rule.

-How your TV is really a display for a variety of picture sources.

Words to know in this chapter:

BAND
COMPONENT
COMPRESSION
DIGITAL VIDEO RECORDERS
DSS/DBS
DUAL LNB"
DUAL TUNER
DVR
P.I.P. , P.O.P. OR SPLIT SCREEN
RADIO WAVES
RF SIGNAL"
SET TOP BOX
SOURCE
UHF
VHF BAND

THE SIGNAL

How the picture gets onto your TV screen

Once you understand how the picture and sound get into your TV set, it will be clear how and why you will choose a particular hook up, and you will be able to work your remote to watch what you want!

The Source of your Picture

What do you want to watch?

Understanding the word "source" in relation to your TV can already help you use a number of remote controls. The **SOURCE** is what your TV is displaying. It can be the 6:00 news, a movie channel, a DVD, a Video Tape, Tommy's first steps on your camcorder or a video game. Each device or component is considered a *source of the picture* which includes the DVD, the Video Tape, the Cable TV or Satellite box, the antenna, etc.

Your sources are either from the OUTSIDE— like Cable TV, Satellite or antenna...

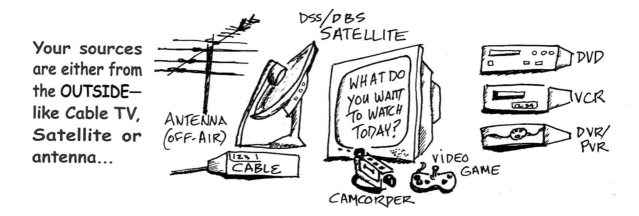

...OR

From a **COMPONENT** that is connected to your TV.

Section 1: Outside Sources

Outside sources include **off-air antenna** broadcasts, **Cable TV**, and **Satellite**. Whether you are watching a local broadcast station, a premium movie channel, or a basic Cable TV or Satellite subscription channel (like CNN), you are bringing the signal to your TV from an outside source.

These signals are sent to your home by **RADIO WAVES** that travel either through the air (as in Broadcast TV that your antenna receives), a cable (from a Cable TV provider), or via Satellite to the dish on your roof.

Signals from many communication devices travel to our homes including telephone, cell phones, radios, walkie-talkies. In the world of invisible signals, there is a range of frequencies where each channel or radio station travel. For example your cell phone travels on a different frequency than your TV.

TV signals are sent on a range of frequencies called bands. (Think "citizen band" or CB radios, that talk to each other at a certain range of frequencies—the citizen's **BAND**.)

Lower frequencies are on the VHF BAND, while those above channel 13 are UHF.

In the U.S., the FCC (Federal Communications Commission) regulates what gets sent at each band so there is enough room for mobile phones, for radio, a place for TV, and for new wireless technologies.

All sound waves are hitting our homes all of the time.

UHF
VHF
FM RADIO
MOBILE PHONES

CHANNEL 53
CHANNEL 28
CHANNEL 13
CHANNEL 2
107.5
95.5
87.1

This is just a sample. There are many more

Understanding the idea of bands of frequencies will make it easier to understand about tuners, High Definition TV, and how to choose quality cables.

Bringin' it on home to you...

The TV station or production company (like Discovery Channel or HBO) has a show to send to you. It could be a live feed like the news or some sports event or a pre-recorded show like a movie or sit-com, documentary, etc. How the signal reaches your TV depends on whether you have an antenna, cable, or a Satellite dish.

LOCAL BROADCAST: OFF-AIR TV TO YOUR ANTENNA

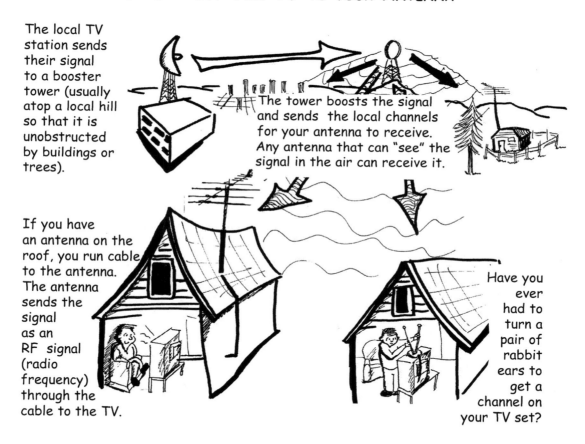

The local TV station sends their signal to a booster tower (usually atop a local hill so that it is unobstructed by buildings or trees).

The tower boosts the signal and sends the local channels for your antenna to receive. Any antenna that can "see" the signal in the air can receive it.

If you have an antenna on the roof, you run cable to the antenna. The antenna sends the signal as an RF signal (radio frequency) through the cable to the TV.

Have you ever had to turn a pair of rabbit ears to get a channel on your TV set?

This will help you to understand: RF inputs, cables, hooking up to antenna cables, tuners, and High Definition TV.

CABLE TV--

The Local TV station or Cable TV production company sends their signal to your local Cable TV company which may serve as many as 400,000 homes.

ALL OF THE STATIONS are sent through fiber optic cables to a hub that serves your city, or about 40,000 homes.

The signal travels through more fiber optic cables from the Distribution Hub to Fiber Nodes which serve your neighborhood, or about 500 homes.

From the Fiber Nodes, the cables may take to the air on telephone poles or be buried underground where they will connect to your home.

If you have premium movie channels or digital cable you need a box to decode the signal.

With Basic Cable TV service, the cable can hook right into your TV set.

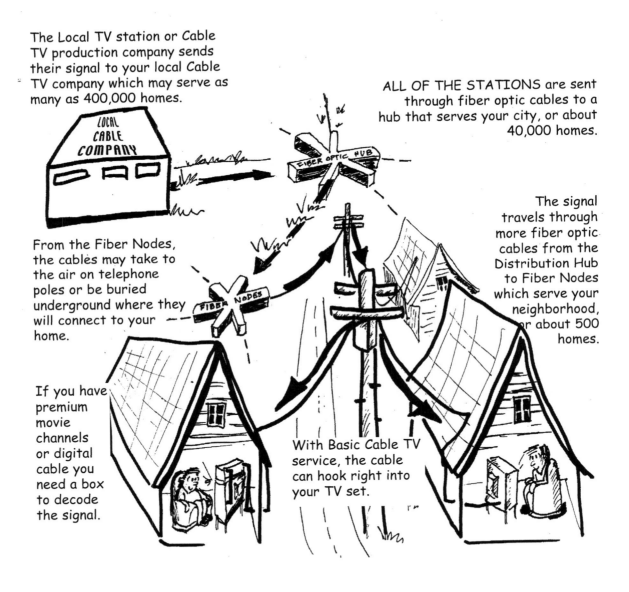

SATELLITE DISH: DSS/DBS

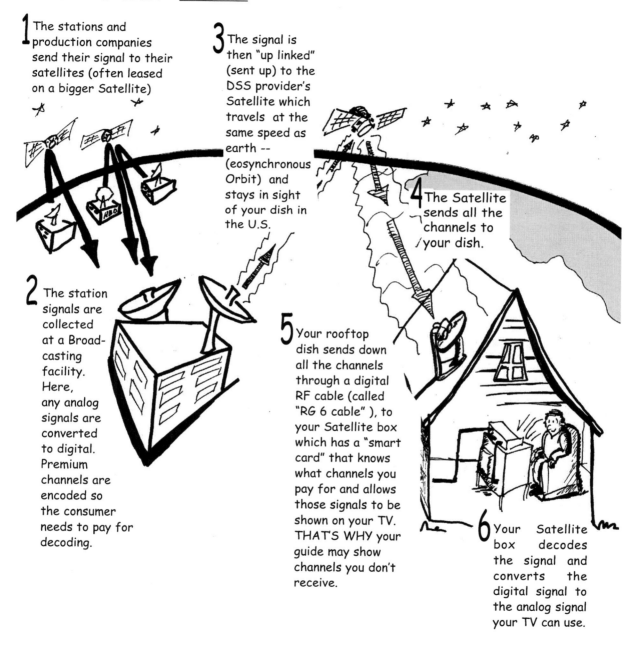

1 The stations and production companies send their signal to their satellites (often leased on a bigger Satellite)

2 The station signals are collected at a Broadcasting facility. Here, any analog signals are converted to digital. Premium channels are encoded so the consumer needs to pay for decoding.

3 The signal is then "up linked" (sent up) to the DSS provider's Satellite which travels at the same speed as earth -- (eosynchronous Orbit) and stays in sight of your dish in the U.S.

4 The Satellite sends all the channels to your dish.

5 Your rooftop dish sends down all the channels through a digital RF cable (called "RG 6 cable"), to your Satellite box which has a "smart card" that knows what channels you pay for and allows those signals to be shown on your TV. THAT'S WHY your guide may show channels you don't receive.

6 Your Satellite box decodes the signal and converts the digital signal to the analog signal your TV can use.

Into your Home and to your TV

Why do you need a Cable TV box or Satellite box?

The Satellite or Cable TV company sends the signals for all the channels to your Satellite dish or TV, but you probably don't see all of those channels. Some channels may be garbled and mixed up.

It doesn't look right to the TV because either...

It's a premium subscription station that the Cable TV company wants to charge a premium for— movie channels and other packages— so the Cable TV company has scrambled up the signal with a special code (encoded signal), and you need a **SET TOP BOX** to unscramble the signal before it gets to your TV.

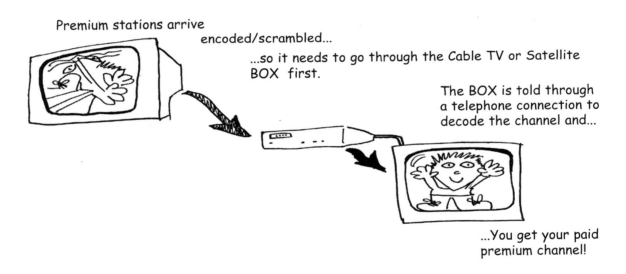

Premium stations arrive encoded/scrambled...

...so it needs to go through the Cable TV or Satellite BOX first.

The BOX is told through a telephone connection to decode the channel and...

...You get your paid premium channel!

OR **because it's a DIGITAL SIGNAL.** It comes in through 1s and 0s. We don't watch 1s and 0s. Just like how a computer changes those 1s and 0s into pictures on our computer monitor. In that same way, the TV can't show pictures because it's not digital. It needs something to translate the digital signal and feed it **ANALOG** pictures. *Note*...some DTV and HDTV sets have a CableCard and can decode subscription channels. This will be discussed in the HDTV chapter.

A digital signal needs to be converted from digital to analog to be displayed on your TV. If it isn't converted, there will be no picture or sound.

So, you see, **you can't just connect your TV to the cable that is receiving a Satellite signal or the digital Cable TV signal or the premium stations Cable TV signal.**

A DIGITAL SIGNAL must be **CONVERTED** to **ANALOG** so that we can enjoy it.

THIS COULDN'T REALLY HAPPEN— But, if we COULD see Digital Codes, it might look like this....

When you have a scrambled or digital signal, you need to hook up the outside line through your Cable TV or Satellite Box. Here the signal can be converted from digital to analog and it can be decoded if needed.

Along with the decoder (translator, descrambler), inside the Cable TV/Satellite box is a tuner.

It unscrambles the stations, but it also **tunes in** to the channel you want to watch.

About Digital and Analog Signals

Satellite and digital Cable TV use digital signals like those of a computer, each piece of information is a 1 or 0 which can be translated into analog — the kind we see and hear. **"Digital Signals" can have different meanings.**

DIGITAL CABLE TV-- Uses digital signals to send more programming (more channels) through the cables. While it is a better picture than regular Cable TV or off-air broadcasts, it has been compressed and expanded, and loses a little quality in the translation.

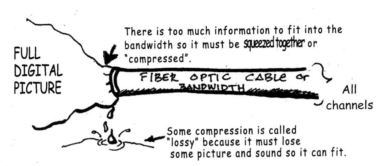

FULL DIGITAL PICTURE

There is too much information to fit into the bandwidth so it must be squeezed together or "compressed".

FIBER OPTIC CABLE or BANDWIDTH

All channels

Some compression is called "lossy" because it must lose some picture and sound so it can fit.

Each channel travels within the given range of channel frequencies so it won't interfere with its neighboring channels.

DIGITAL SATELLITE- Uses digital signals with less **COMPRESSION** and offers a better quality picture.

DIGITAL TV OR HDTV-Uses a different band to send out digital signals which can remain digital into a DIGITAL TV, or is converted to analog in a High Definition set top box. There is a wider bandwidth for each station which allows more information — better sound and picture — to be sent, received, and viewed. To receive the quality of Digital TV, the set must be "HD ready" and capable of showing all the information. A traditional analog TV may be able to receive signals from an HDTV set top tuner if it has the right connections but will not be able to show the High Definition quality picture or sound. More about this in the HDTV chapter.

SO, you don't need a Digital TV to view Digital Cable TV or Satellite signals, but you do need a digital or HDTV to get the high definition quality of HDTV.

Now you can see that "digital Cable TV" or "digital Satellite" are still used for traditional TVs and "Digital TV" or "HDTV" requires a new kind of TV, And that not all digital signals carry the same quality picture and sound.

SECTION 2: The Tuner

A **TUNER** is used to change the channel to what you want to watch. All the stations that your equipment is capable of receiving are available to your TV in that band of frequencies that your TV receives. Each station's signal comes in on a channel. Each channel is received on different frequencies within the VHF/UHF band. Think of tuning in to a radio station that actually uses its frequency in its call letters—KLOS 95.5 is at 95.5 MHz frequency. To view a TV channel, the tuner picks the frequency of that channel.

Simple stuff. Inside your TV there is a tuner. When you change the channel, it **tunes in** to the frequency of that channel.

BASIC CABLE TV OR ANTENNA

When you change the channel, the tuner receives the frequency of that channel. It points to the place (frequency) in the VHF or UHF band that carries that channel.

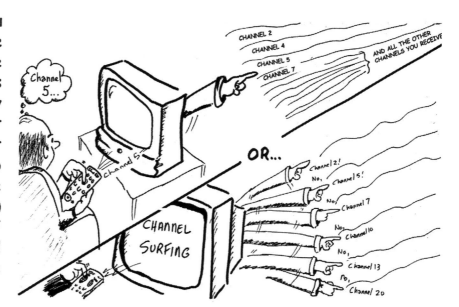

When you have a Cable TV box or Satellite box, you use its tuner and bypass the tuner in the TV.

A set top box has its own tuner to change the channels and you tell that Cable TV or Satellite box what channel to watch (usually using your remote). It now sends only that signal to your TV set.

Your TV set has nothing to do but show the signal. If you tried to change the channel on the TV, it wouldn't work because you *are not using the TV tuner.*

Cable TV or Satellite Box

One tuner can only tune into one channel.** It decodes and/or converts the signal of the channel to which you are tuned, and then sends it on to the next component --VCR, DVR, — to the TV.

To receive two stations, you would need another box, or another tuner. To get three channels you would need three.

If you have a Cable TV or Satellite box with one tuner, you *can* hook up more than one TV but you'll have to watch the same thing on all the TV's hooked up to that box. This may not be a bad thing if you live alone because additional boxes usually have additional monthly charges. Watching the same station on an additional TV is called a ***"slave"***. The main TV is the ***"master"*** who tells the slave what they will watch --not unlike a parent and child....

SO, if you want Cable TV or Satellite on more than one TV *and* you want to be able to watch more than one show at the same time, **you need a separate Cable TV box / Satellite receiver for each additional station you want to watch.**

There are exceptions. New Satellite receiver and DVR combinations have two tuners which can be shared on more than one TV. Still, it follows the rule...

...You need one tuner for each channel you want to watch.

Dual Tuners

You have probably seen **P.I.P.** , **P.O.P.** or **SPLIT SCREEN** listed as features on some TVs. A single tuner TV can show the picture from another component (which, if it is a Cable TV box or VCR, will have a tuner to show a second channel). **DUAL TUNER** TVs can show a second channel in the box with the Picture in Picture or split screen, and it uses its own second tuner to change the channel (if it is basic Cable TV or a signal that doesn't require a set top box).

Other components have dual tuners. Some satellites boxes with **DIGITAL VIDEO RECORDERS –"DVR"** have 2 tuners in the same unit. The second tuner on a Satellite box/digital video recorder or web TV allows you to watch one program while recording another or you can record two programs at the same time.

TV WITH "2 TUNER PICTURE IN PICTURE"

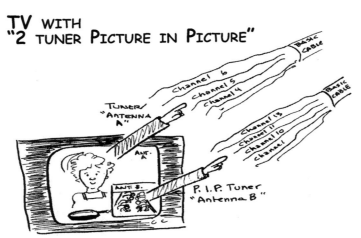

TV tuners cannot unscramble premium channels. To use 2 tuner P.I.P., the signal on both inputs needs to be antenna or basic Cable TV. (except on "Digital Cable Ready" sets see HDTV chapter.)

If you have Satellite or digital Cable TV, you would need a separate set top box for each channel you want to see (and you would change the channel on the set top box). 2 tuner P.I.P. is useless with Satellite or digital Cable TV

SATELLITE AND DVR COMBINATION WITH DUAL TUNERS

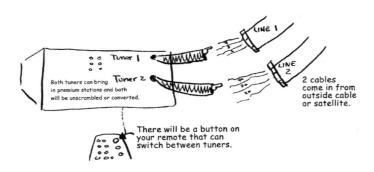

Each Satellite tuner input must have a separate cable from the Satellite. (See exception that follows) You cannot split the signal like you can on basic Cable TV or antenna.

To receive two or more signals from your Satellite dish, you must use a Satellite dish with **"DUAL LNB"** that is, it receives two signals that it can send out. "Dual LNB" dishes can split signals to more than 2 TVs with the use of a "multiplexer" usually installed by your Satellite installer.

Dual Tuner Satellite or Cable TV Box with DVR

You can now find Satellite receivers and Cable TV boxes with built in DVRs (digital video recorder) that allow you to record programming onto a hard drive. Many of them feature pause and rewind capabilities as you watch live TV. A great benefit of the combination unit is that you can watch one program while you record another, or even record two programs at the same time. This is because there are two lines feeding into the unit with a tuner picking a channel from each incoming line. It can handle subscription channels as well as basic package channels on both tuners.

Until 2004, the basic premise of needing a separate box for each TV was true. Satellite manufacturers are making units that can share its incoming signals as well as anything recorded on the unit. It can record up to two programs and/or play back two programs all at the same time, and it can do it on more than one TV! Echostar (DISH network), does this with a special cable hookup to the second TV along with a remote control dedicated to the second TV. This hookup will require professional installers through DISH. If you are interested..the box uses existing in-home room-to-room cables. It sends the signal from the receiver (rather than it coming from outside) to the second TV through an unused UHF channel. The second remote control works on an RF (radio frequency) so it can control the receiver from another room. You press the remote in the other room and can watch either a Satellite channel or a recorded show.

The Satellite box has dual tuners.

Each TV can access one tuner (watch different channels) or it can watch recorded shows stored on the box.

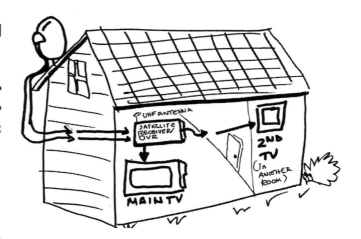

A second remote can tell the DVR to record a TV show without leaving the 2nd room.

Note: Newer models will accept 1 cable from the dish and split the signal to the 2 tuners internally.
New technologies will change this even more.

SECTION 3: The Antenna Connection on your TV...

When you hook up the cable from the wall jack into your TV, you will connect it to a screw-like connection on the back of your TV, usually labeled "antenna".

The TV says to itself "Hey, I have a signal and I'll be able to change channels because it's feeding my tuner". This signal is called an **"RF SIGNAL"**, as the tuner finds the radio frequency for each channel.

But wait!
If you have a Cable TV or Satellite box, you know that you use its tuner. You have to tell the TV tuner to take a break and not look for a signal...

...That's why you put your TV on Channel 3
(And in some cases channel 4)

If you put the TV on channel 3, and you hook the cable into the antenna input, the TV will accept whatever picture it is being fed. The TV is passive–you are bypassing the tuner– and you are free to change channels on the Cable TV/Satellite box tuner.

If you forget, and change the channel on the TV, you will not receive the picture from the Satellite or Cable TV box. The TV tuner will look for a picture on another channel but there will be nothing because the signal is coming in where channel 3 would be.

A Word About VCRs...

VCRs have tuners too! In a basic setup with an antenna or basic Cable TV, the VCR will use its tuner to change the channel to record what you want.

The VCR cannot unscramble or convert digital signals. Premium and Digital stations will still need a set-top box. And, remember, if you use a Satellite or Cable TV box-- their tuners rule. You will hook up the outside line to the Cable TV box and from the box to the VCR antenna in. Now, you also put the VCR on channel 3, and again, change channels on the Cable TV or Satellite box. This means you have to make sure the Cable TV/Satellite box on the channel you want to record.

Some VCRs have a feature that will change the channel on the Cable TV box when you want to record. This works through an IR adapter. That is the same way your remote control changes the channel on your equipment. It simply passes the signal on from the VCR. The VCR stays on channel 3 or the same input so that it continues to receive the signal.

For BASIC Cable TV OR ANTENNA— The VCR uses its tuner to change channels. The TV is on Channel 3.

A CABLE TV OR SATELLITE BOX uses its tuner. Now BOTH the VCR AND the TV are on Channel 3.

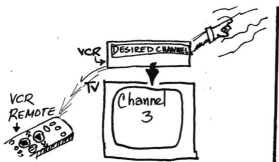

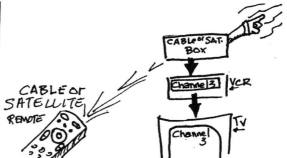

A Cable TV Box controller simply passes on the channel changing instructions to the Cable TV box, the same way the remote control sends the signal to the VCR (via INFRARED signal or "IR").

ANOTHER THING ABOUT VCRs: PASS-THROUGH SIGNAL

When you hook up your VCR, it will come between the signal from the wall or Cable TV Satellite box and your TV. That is, the cable will go into the VCR and then out of the VCR to your TV. This works with the coaxial, RF, antenna cable. (On Super VHS decks it can also work with S-Video connections, but more on that later).

You may have noticed that you don't need to turn on the power of the VCR for the signal to go through. That is because the VCR is set up like a tunnel to just send the signal right on through...

...UNTIL YOU TURN ON THE VCR. When you turn on the VCR, it hangs onto the signal. When you try to watch your TV, often there will be interference, fuzz, or even no picture.

That's where the **TV/VTR button** comes in. In the **TV position,** the pass-through is available. This will work on antenna and basic Cable TV. It tells the VCR to let the signal pass through, that you don't want to watch what the VCR is recording. Remember, if you have a Cable TV or Satellite box, you won't be able to watch another channel than what is recording because the VCR can't use its own tuner and must use the Cable TV or Satellite box tuner.

To watch what the VCR is recording or to watch a video tape, Press the TV/VTR button to the **VTR position.** Now the TV displays what the VCR is "seeing", whether it is a TV station signal or a tape that is being played.

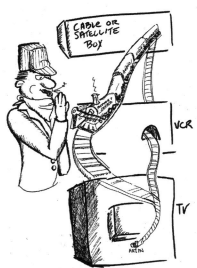

This will help you to understand why you can't see a picture or have bad reception when you have your TV hooked up in-line with the VCR.

Understanding that a signal passes through the VCR (or an audio/video home theater receiver) will help you to understand how to hook up your equipment.

SECTION 4: Other Sources – Components

Most people don't watch TV programming all of the time. Sometimes you want to watch a movie or other recorded programs. When watching something other than a broadcast signal, the TV becomes a monitor which shows whatever signal the source is playing and does not use its tuner.

Usually these components are hooked up through inputs, connections other than the antenna connection (exceptions will be discussed in the hookup preparation chapter). These other video input connections bypass the TV tuner altogether.

Remember that you use channel 3 (or 4) to display components that are hooked into the antenna connection. To watch another input on your TV, you will have to change the TV to the INPUT connected to that SOURCE or DEVICE.

**When you decide to use one of your TV's inputs (not just the antenna connection), you have a bigger choice of cables and connections.
This allows you to choose better quality sound and picture.**

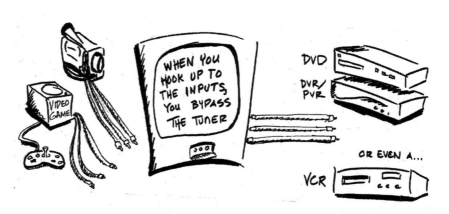

Front inputs are convenient for devices that you want to connect and disconnect like camcorders or video game consoles.

Types of Components

VIDEO RECORDERS -

VCR: Though it probably needs little explanation, this device records programs onto a magnetic video tape. This device works by recording an analog signal onto a tape. High definition digital VHS records a digital signal on magnetic tape. Video tapes must be rewound and fast forwarded to the place on the tape where the signal was physically recorded. VCRs can be combined with TVs or DVDs.

Photo courtesy of Samsung.

VCR/DVD COMBINATION: This component was designed as a space saver. For people who did not have an extra shelf (or want another piece of equipment), manufacturers combined an old fashioned VCR and a DVD player in the same device. It works in the same way it would if they were separate devices. The VCR still works to tape broadcast shows and video fed in through a cable from camcorders, other VCRs, or any other source that feeds it a picture. The biggest thing to know here is that YOU **CANNOT COPY A DVD ONTO A VIDEOTAPE.** The copyright protection that does not allow you to copy from a stand alone DVD to a stand alone VCR will also stop you from recording on combination units.

DVR (ALSO CALLED "PVR", "HDD" OR "HARD DISC RECORDER"):

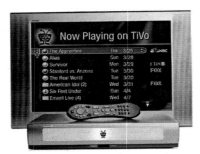

photo © TiVo® Inc. All Rights Reserved.

This device is called a Digital Video Recorder or Personal Video Recorder or sometimes simply a hard disc recorder. It uses a hard disc drive like the one found on your computer to record programs. Typically, you choose the program you want to record from an on-screen guide. Some DVRs allow you to choose to record a whole season of your favorite programs with simple menus. You do not have to tell the PVR/DVR when the show is on, it receives that information through a phone line or the Satellite/Cable TV provider. Once recorded on the hard drive it can be saved to a VHS tape if it is connected to a VCR. Programs can be saved or deleted to use the available memory. A DVR also will automatically record the last 30 minutes of the channel which you have tuned to, whether your TV is powered on or not. This allows you to pause or rewind "live TV". Once you change the channel, the "live TV" memory is wiped clean and the 30 minutes begin again. The benefit of this device is that you can also start to watch a program from its beginning even if the program is not yet done recording.

Photo courtesy of Dish Network, Echostar Communications

SATELLITE or CABLE BOX & PVR (DVR) COMBINATION:
These combinations typically have 2 tuners so that you can record two channels at the same time, or watch one and record another. When combined with a Satellite or digital Cable TV box, the signal is not converted from digital to analog until it leaves the box to go to the TV. This means that it can record more hours of programming because the compressed digital signal takes up less space on the hard drive than an analog signal would. Often the Satellite or Cable TV provider will install this for you as you will often need a second line brought into your home. New features allow for Video-On-Demand. Usually the Cable TV or Satellite box will record shows or channels for you to choose to watch at your convenience. It does not typically occupy the same space on the hard drive that you use to make your own recordings.

DVD RECORDER:
Thanks again to the computer world, this device allows you to record onto a DVD like you would record onto a VHS tape. The various names of this device refers to different formats used by different manufacturers. At this time some of the formats are not able to be played on machines by other manufacturers, but it all should soon be compatible. The DVD-RW format allows you to erase previous recordings and re-record on the same DVD (as you would on a vhs tape). Because this is a digital medium , you can access any place on the disc (like going to the song you want on a CD). This also has allowed some machines to "time shift" record. Like a PVR, with Time Shift you can start watching a show from the beginning after the show has started recording, or you can play back a show already recorded on the DVD while the DVD records another at the same time.

Photo courtesy of LG Electronics.

DVD RECORDER & VCR COMBINATION:
This component has both a recordable DVD and a VHS *player*. It will allow you to record a broadcast program onto DVD and it will allow you to copy what you have on Videotape to a DVD. This means you can take the home movies or previously recorded VHS tapes, and copy them to DVD. This is a better quality format and gives you the advantage of digital access. You will now be able to jump to Little Tommy's first steps or your cousin's wedding that has been transferred onto the DVD.

DVR (PVR) & DVD RECORDER COMBINATION:

This device is a Digital Video Recorder that will record your programming onto a hard disc as it is with a stand alone PVR/DVR. The addition of the DVD recorder on this machine allows you to then choose to archive (save for the future) your programs onto a DVD to be watched on another DVD player or just to be watched in the future. By transferring the programs to DVD, you can delete them from the DVR's hard drive and free up space for future programs.

WATCHING MOVIES –

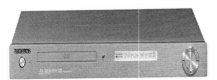

Photos courtesy of Samsung.

DVD:

A component that allows you to play DVDs and CDs. DVD stands for Digital Versatile Disc which refers to the way you can jump around different scenes or chapters on a recorded DVD. Because it is digital, it has better quality than the Analog Video Tape. The DVD has a built in DAC (digital to analog converter) so that its programming can be watched on an Analog, NTSC TV. Some DVDs have features for playing music in surround sound. Examples are SACD (created by Sony) and DVD Audio. The music discs are special premium discs encoded for this kind of play and the DVD must be connected to a home theater receiver through an analog 6 channel audio configuration.

LASERDISC PLAYER:

This was the predecessor to DVDs. It is a large disc the size of an old record album which was used to show the first digital movies. Rarely are laserdisc players available now because few movies are made on them, but the explanation is given for those of you who have loved ones who bought them and may still own them. Some video purists believe the quality of Laserdiscs are better than the typical DVD because there is less compression.

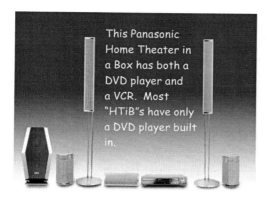

This Panasonic Home Theater in a Box has both a DVD player and a VCR. Most "HTiB"'s have only a DVD player built in.

HOME THEATER WITH BUILT IN DVD ("HTiB"s: "HOME THEATER IN A BOX"):

Home theater is growing in popularity due to surround sound on DVDs, Satellite and digital broadcasting. Home theater requires a stereo or audio/video receiver to send out the sound to 5 speakers and a bass speaker unit. (See HDTV chapter section on audio). Because manufacturers understand that people want a space-saving, all-in-one , easy-to-hook-up-and-use solution for home theater, they have created receivers that have a built in DVD player. With this unit you can play CDs or DVDs. Often there is a built-in radio tuner and sometimes you can add other music components (like a tape player, mini-disc or other audio or music source).

OTHER SOURCES TO WATCH –

CAMCORDERS: Listed here as a source to hook up to your TV to view your home movies. Camcorders record home movies onto video tapes either compact vhs tapes, 8 mm, high 8, digital tapes, mini-dv (for digi-cams) and now even recorded straight to DVD or a memory card. A camcorder can be connected to a TV input and displayed. A front connection/input is helpful to hook up a camcorder as you will want to hook it up and remove it without reaching behind the TV. Some VCRs and DVD recorders have front inputs so that you can copy your movies onto video tape. If you hook it up through the VCR, it can then be displayed on the TV by choosing the VCR input. On your VCR you will have to choose the front input to watch the camcorder's tape.

DIGITAL CAMERAS WITH VIDEO HOOKUP: Many of today's digital cameras come with a connection to the camera which has a yellow RCA connector on the other end. For these cameras, you can hook it into your TV and display the photos on your camera much like a slide show.

VIDEO GAME CONSOLES:
Nintendo®, Sony Playstations®, Xbox or other, this is the device that your children or grandchildren, (or neighbor's kids) can't seem to get enough of. Controllers allow you to interact with the game, making characters run, jump, fly, attack and blow things up. Video games are best hooked up to front jacks for easy removal. A word of Caution: **CONSULT YOUR MANUAL BEFORE USING VIDEO GAMES ON A REAR PROJECTION TV or PLASMA TV !** The games often have a static background that can burn a permanent image onto the TV screen if displayed for the typical length of time that kids play them.

WEB TV or INTERNET DEVICE:
This device was popular as the internet came into the homes of people who did not want a computer but wanted the access (or wanted the access on their TV). More often the online features of Web TV have been incorporated into video games consoles like "X box" for online gaming, or other combinations with DVRs, or other Media Center type units.

COMPUTER:
The computer has inspired many of the advances in home entertainment products from hard disc drives in DVRs, to displaying slide shows on DVD players. As technology advances it seems that more home entertainment products will "network" (connect and talk) with your home computer. This has been called "**convergence**". Your digital photos, home movies, and music can be displayed on your TV and played through your home theater sound system.

MEDIA CENTER:
Technology designers noticed that there were many similarities between home entertainment components and computers, like DVD players, and hard drives. Media Centers promise "all in one" components. They will record TV like a DVR, and they will play and record ("burn") DVDs and CDs. Some media centers are labeled "entertainment PCs," others are manufactured by home entertainment manufacturers. One benefit of a media center is that it is dedicated to audio and video and will be able to send "streaming video" which will send real time video without stuttering like a home computer that is doing other tasks at the same time as entertaining you.

What you should know is that the line between your home computer and your home entertainment system is blurring and that there are many who believe that the direction of technology is to ultimately merge the internet and TV programming providers so that you will have video on demand from the internet. We have a little way to go before it comes together.

Digital and High Definition TV

WHAT YOU WILL LEARN IN CHAPTER 2...

-How TVs have evolved.

-What is HDTV?

-How and when the transition to HDTV will affect you.

-The difference between NTSC and ATSC.

-The difference between analog and digital TV.

-What is the difference between SDTV, EDTV & HDTV.

-How a TV works.

-What is progressive scan and what is interlaced?

-How to get a good picture from an Analog NTSC
   signal on an HDTV.

-How to choose your next TV.

 -What is the difference between an HDTV and an
    HD-ready TV.

-The difference between types of HDTVs and how to choose one.

-How you receive HDTV today from Antenna, Satellite or Cable TV.

 -What you'll need in order to receive HDTV.

-What is Dolby Digital® and DTS™ 5.1 surround sound and how it is
   different from TV sound of the past.

Words to know in this chapter:

3:2 PULLDOWN.
5.1 CHANNEL SURROUND SOUND
AC-3
ARTIFACTS
ASPECT RATIO
ATSC
BETAMAX ACT
BURN-IN
CABLECARD
CATHODE RAY TUBE
CONVERGENCE
CRT
DAC
DCR
DE-INTERLACER
DIGITAL CABLE READY
DIGITAL LIGHT PROCESSOR
DIGITAL MICROMIRROR DEVICE
DIRECT VIEW
"DISCRETE" CHANNELS
DLP™
DMD
DOLBY DIGITAL®
DOLBY PRO-LOGIC®
DTS®
DVD-AUDIO
FIELD
FIXED PIXEL DISPLAY
FPS
FRAME
FRONT PROJECTION TV
HD READY
HDCP
HDTV
HOME THEATER

HORIZONTAL RESOLUTION
INTEGRATED TUNERS
INTERLACED
ISF CERTIFIED
LCD
LCOS
LENTICULAR SCREEN
LINE DOUBLERS
LIQUID CRYSTAL DISPLAY
MBPS
MULTICASTING
NTSC D/A CONVERTERS
"OTA"
PERSISTENCE OF VISION
PHOSPHORS
PIXEL
PLASMA
PROGRESSIVE SCAN
REAR SCREEN PROJECTION
RESOLUTION
RPTV
SACD
SIMULCAST
TIME SHIFTING
TRANSMISSIVE
UPCONVERT

Section 1: The History of Television

There is much confusion over **HDTV** and when, how, and *if* the transition will happen. To understand the plans for the future, we need to see how we got to the invention of HDTV and the **ATSC**. History? Politics? Understanding why choices were made helps to make sense of how things work.

From Invention to today...

Back in the 1930s, TV began broadcasting to households. The black and white signal was sent to big boxes with small picture tubes. In the beginning the RMA (Radio Manufacturers Association) told broadcasters and manufacturers how the signals would be sent and received: brightness, shape of picture, and synchronization—how it is displayed. It allotted a spectrum of radio frequencies so TV tuners could receive the signal and would not interfere with radio signals. (See "Getting the Picture" chapter 1).

On March 8, 1941, a single standard was devised so that manufacturers of TVs, broadcasters, and everyone else involved in sending and receiving TV signals would be set up in the same way and all of the equipment would all understand and display the signals. These standards were set by the **NTSC** (National Television Standards Committee). Broadcasters sent this analog picture and sound signal via radio frequency waves through the air. In order to insure that the different TV stations didn't run into each other, a cushion of frequencies was allotted between each station. This way channel 4 didn't interfere with channel 5. When color was added to broadcasts in the 1950's (adopted widely in the 1960s), the NTSC standards ensured that black and white televisions would not become obsolete, continuing to receive signals and display black and white pictures even though they were broadcast in color.

Over the years, more TV stations sprang up. They needed more frequencies to send out the signals for the increasing number of channels. The Federal Communications Commission (FCC) allotted more bandwidth to cover these additional stations in an Ultra High Frequency (UHF) range or spectrum. Cable TV added even more channels. Mobile phones, FM radio, ham radios, the internet and more, all needed a frequency to send their signals through the airwaves. The amount of space in the radio wave frequency was getting crowded and spectrum became valuable.

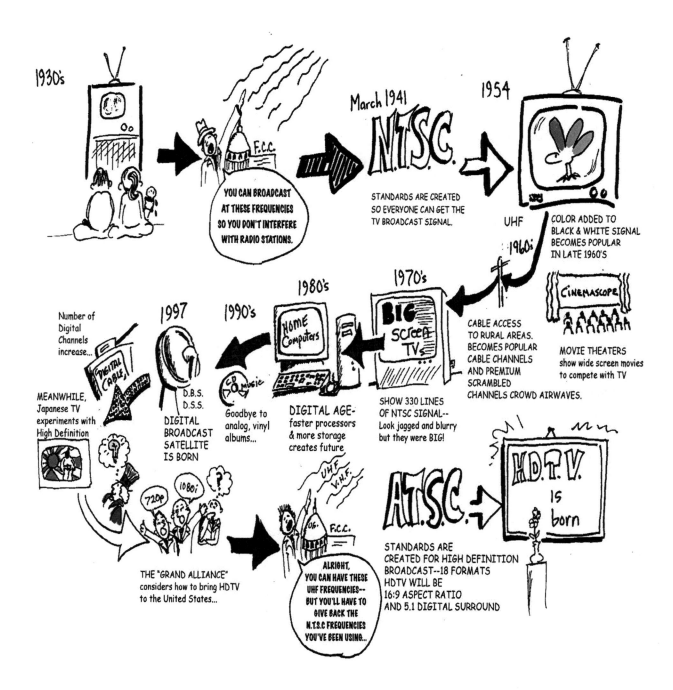

Our Current System:

NTSC stands for National Television System Committee. This group created standards for Television broadcasts so that all TVs could receive the signal. The NTSC created today's standards in the 1950s when color television was announced.

NOTE: There are two other standards in the world, PAL and SECAM. Because televisions in other countries may be setup differently than those in the U.S., VCRs, videotapes and DVDs purchased in other countries may not be playable on your TV at home. (See Appendix for list of PAL and SECAM countries.)

How the "digital age" has changed TV

With the invention of computers, old analog signals could now be turned into digital 1's and 0's—the same way a computer creates the image displayed on a computer monitor. As technology made computer silicon chips smaller, faster, and less expensive to produce, it changed the way that audio and video could be recorded and transmitted and was finally integrated into your home electronics. With digital compression , more information and more channels could be sent. (See "About Digital and Analog Signals" in chapter 1.)

Analog signals could now be "digitized". Computers could convert analog signals. Then the digital signals could be converted back to analog signals and displayed on your TV. **D/A CONVERTERS** (read as "D to A"), or "**DAC**" could be made small enough for even portable CD players. Digital sound came into our lives. As computer chips and processors evolved, video was able to be converted to digital as well, resulting in the DVD.

CONVERTING ANALOG TO DIGITAL AND DIGITAL TO ANALOG
OR HOW SOUND AND PICTURE BECOME 1'S AND 0'S AND BACK AGAIN (DACs)

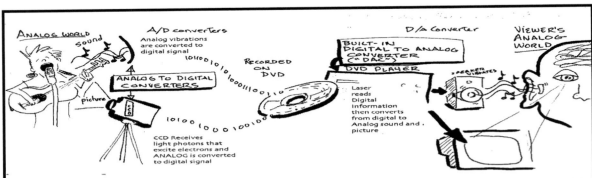

Vinyl albums and analog cassette tapes were abandoned as analog to digital converters could turn music into digital information on a CD. Today picture and sound are captured, converted to digital signals and recorded onto a DVD. DVD players , a/v receivers, DVRs, and some TVs have "digital to analog converters" so we can watch them as the picture and sound we recognize.

Digital processors like those in your computer made it possible to deliver a better picture. Digital signals could be compressed, squeezed together, then sent to your home, and expanded again on the other side. Home receivers converted and decoded these signals and sent them to your TV as an analog signal. Because the digital signals take up less space and could be made smaller by compressing them, more information could be sent as a digital signal. More TV stations could be sent. More information meant better picture and more sound than traditional analog NTSC signals.

ANALOG CHANNEL TRANSMISSION COMPARED TO DIGITAL CHANNEL
HOW DIGITAL CAN SQUEEZE MORE INFORMATION IN THE SAME CHANNEL SPACE.

Analog signals can interfere with neighboring channels. Part of the NTSC bandwidth is used to give each channel a buffer, so only 4.2 MHz, out of the allotted 6 MHz, can be used for picture. The result is 330 horizontal lines out of a possible 525 on an NTSC TV. Which means lower picture quality.

Digital signals can be compressed so that more information can be sent in about the same bandwidth as old analog NTSC. ATSC can send 1,080 horizontal lines of picture. (See "About Digital & Analog Signals" in Chapter 1)

Digital bandwidth is measured like internet connections in bits per second (**Mbps**) Each broadcaster is allotted about 19.39 Mbps which they can use for any combination of digital TV, HDTV, or multiple channels.

ATSC is born...

With the possibility of sending more information in the same amount of space, there came an opportunity to make the quality of the picture on your TV almost as good as a film you may see in your local theater. Big screen televisions and surround sound opened the door to have a theater at home ("**HOME THEATER**"). In the 1980s Japan developed transmission of a high quality analog broadcast. U.S. broadcasters and manufacturers, impressed with the picture quality wanted to bring the technology to U.S. TV. Rather than use old analog broadcasts, they chose to take advantage of new digital broadcast capabilities.

In 1993, a group of filmmakers, broadcasters, and technicians formed the "Grand Alliance". Members of the Grand Alliance included innovators from General Instrument, Zenith, RCA, the Massachusetts Institute of Technology (M.I.T.), AT&T, and Philips. The FCC gave them the task of creating standards for this new High Definition Technology.

Understanding that the ATSC signals are sent over UHF frequencies, makes it easy to remember that you need only a UHF antenna to receive HDTV. You still have to live where you can receive the local stations over the air. (See off-air broadcast illustration in Tuner chapter.)

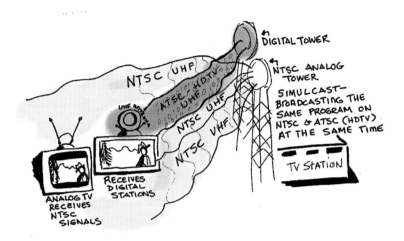

TV programming will be simulcast (broadcast at the same time) on the existing NTSC spectrum and on the new ATSC (HDTV) frequencies.

The FCC licensed a part of unused UHF spectrum to develop and broadcast the new High Definition format. By using available UHF frequencies, the old NTSC signals could be "**SIMULCAST**" (broadcast at the same time) on their current analog channels and digital transmission would be sent on the new UHF channels.

With this new spectrum and new technology, new standards had to be agreed upon. The ATSC–Advanced Television Standards Committee–was formed. They all agreed on a standard for audio, and agreed on 18 specific formats that fit into categories (listed in HDTV formats" chart in Section 3 of this chapter.) All digital TVs would have to be able to receive all formats (and convert them to the TVs format) so that you could watch the program. HDTVs would have to display at high definition resolutions.

The company that creates the technology that becomes the standard will profit from the licensing by other manufacturers. That's why there is so much confusion and competing formats when new technology is introduced.

The road has not been smooth. It is confusing to consumers to hear of disagreements in standards and some people may have wondered if HDTV was going to happen at all. It was the same when color TV came into being; there were different opinions of how to best create this new picture. Which format is best? Which technology? The winner of which standard would be adopted stood to profit. It would be like winning the licensing lottery. With each innovation, TVs, set top tuners, high definition DVDs, each manufacturer lobbies for their technology to be the standard. It slows down the process. (Think of how VHS won out over Sony's Betamax tapes in the 1980s.) As in the past, the FCC has worked with manufacturers to ensure that the set you buy today will work with whatever standard is created tomorrow. **This will assure you that new technologies will not make your equipment obsolete.**

Enter the Hollywood Studios

Digital copies can be perfect copies, and like the music industry, movie studios did not want to lose revenue from pirated copies of their movies.

Along with delays caused by competing manufacturers , another problem had to be solved for those who created the content that would be sent on digital TV. The concerns of Hollywood had to be taken into account so that the transition to HDTV could progress. This is where the filmmaker and the manufacturer must agree on content protection technologies.

PERFECT DIGITAL COPIES

With an analog signal, like NTSC, each copy loses a little quality from the signal from which it is copied. With a digital signal, the 1s and 0s don't change from original to copy. (Just like a copy of a computer document is exactly the same as the original). This means the copy will be as good as the signal you feed into the device that can record it.

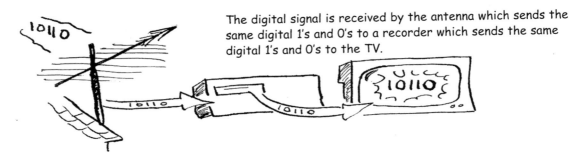

The digital signal is received by the antenna which sends the same digital 1's and 0's to a recorder which sends the same digital 1's and 0's to the TV.

An analog copy tends to be darker and grainy...

...whereas a digital copy is perfect

So, you can see that if you can copy a digital signal like a DVD, digital TV or HDTV signal, you have a program that could be as good as the original. This makes the filmmakers nervous, but then, they have a history of being nervous about copying programming...

THE BETAMAX DECISION OF 1984: THE "FAIR USE" RULE

When Betamax and VCRs were first sold, Hollywood felt that copying a TV broadcast was copyright infringement. It was considered piracy, or stealing content. Universal Pictures and Disney Studios filed suit against Sony to stop manufacturing recording devices.

The Supreme Court recognized that most copying was for personal use. "**TIME SHIFTING**" (watching a show at a time more convenient for the viewer), and other private use recording was ruled to be considered "fair use". The average viewer would not have to pay for this right.

The filmmakers argued that they would lose money; however, in 2002, home video sales accounted for 60% of Hollywood's revenue.

A passionate debate in 1984 lead Jack Valenti, President of the Motion Picture Association to declare
"I say to you that the VCR is to the American film producer and the American public as the Boston strangler is to the woman home alone."

Much of the confusion about HDTV has come about as the manufacturers, broadcasters and studios have struggled to protect the rights of the artists and studios who create what we watch.

The supreme court ruled that people should be able to "timeshift" programming— to record a broadcast to watch at a time more convenient for the viewer.

COPY PROTECTION: THE SOLUTION

To ease the fears of the filmmakers, manufacturers agreed to build copy protection into their products. For VHS and DVD the copy protection used is commonly "Macrovision". With copy protection like Macrovision, a picture will be scrambled when you try to copy it. What's more, many recording devices like VCRs will scramble copy protected signals that it receives. **That's why you cannot hook up a DVD player to your VCR; the picture will be scrambled.**

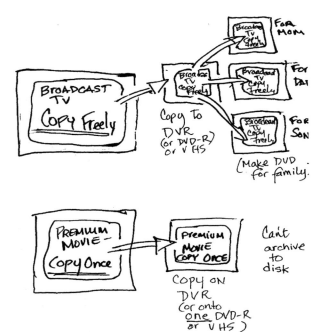

BROADCAST TV
Copy Freely

Broadcast TV copy freely FOR MOM

Broadcast TV copy freely FOR DAD

Broadcast TV copy freely FOR SON

Copy to DVR (or DVD-R) or VHS

(Make DVD for family.)

PREMIUM MOVIE — Copy Once

Premium Movie Copy Once

Can't archive to disk

COPY ON DVR (or onto one DVD-R or VHS)

COPY NOT AT ALL

When a cable carries a digital signal, quality is near perfect . Filmmakers fear it will promote piracy. Manufacturers developed connections to satisfy the broadcasters and filmmakers copy protection needs. The FCC is ensuring that current connections will not become obsolete.

A High Definition picture has near film-like quality! This worried filmmakers, and the argument was resurrected. While the **BETAMAX ACT** of 1984 held that it is legal to copy for personal use, High Definition VCRs and DVRs made it possible for the average consumer to make multiple copies with no loss of quality. Filmmakers again feared that many copies of their show would be shared among networks of friends. They believed they would lose DVD sales. How could both the rights of the viewer and the rights of the filmmakers be satisfied?

In 2003, filmmakers and electronics manufacturers agreed to copy protection. Digital hookups that allow copy protection are becoming the standard. HDMI and DVI cables use a copy protection called **"HDCP"** (high definition copy protection). (See digital connections and cables in the following chapters). iEEE1394 cable ("firewire", "iLink" or "DTVLink") use a copy protections standard called "5C".

Copy protection encoding rules have been put into place. Copy protection embeds a code into a program that allows you to **copy freely** —for basic Cable TV and broadcast TV; or **copy** — premium movie stations; or **no copying** --for Pay Per View events. While this may feel prohibitive, we must understand that movie piracy, like music piracy has caused a loss of profits for the content providers and artists who make the films. "Broadcast flags" are another copyright protection encoding. Broadcast flags prohibit the distribution of programming over the internet (as they try to avoid video file sharing and piracy over the internet like in the days of music sharing on web sites). Many discussions are still taking place. The FCC continues to monitor the situation so that newer technologies won't make existing hookups or equipment obsolete.

The Future of TV

Rest assured. HDTV and ATSC broadcasts are a done deal. When the clock strikes 12:00 on December 31, 2006 the old NTSC spectrum that had been used since the 1930s may turn into a pumpkin. The NTSC spectrum is to be returned to the FCC to license for new technologies. To protect consumers the date is not fixed. The NTSC transmission will only be turned off once "85% of households receive HDTV". But what does "receives HDTV" mean? Currently almost all homes can receive an HD signal from either antenna, Satellite, or Cable TV. Delaying the cutoff date will slow adoption of HDTV and delay the return of the badly needed bandwidth that can be used for new technologies like faster internet or new wireless technologies. (Even microwave ovens use bandwidth!) Note: The following time lines are current as of this book's publication, you may want to track the updates in the news or by going to www.ce.org (the Consumer Electronics Association).

As more older TVs are replaced, and as new TVs are required to be HDTV compatible, the number of households with HDTV will rise to the 85% required before the traditional analog NTSC signal is turned off.

In 2004, the turn off date was considered a "goal" more than a deadline. It seems to be in fluctuation to protect consumers and yet gain back the bandwidth required for new technologies. Your best bet is to plan for the turn off and move to HDTV with your next purchase.

So, how is the change to HDTV going to happen?

The Transition to HDTV-- A Timeline

To ensure that the transition moves forward, former FCC chairman, Michael Powell, created the "Powell Plan" as a guide for deadlines toward making the transition to HDTV a reality. The following is that timeline: By the time you read this, it will probably change.
Check our website: **www.home-electronics-survival.com** *for the newest deadlines.*

JANUARY 2003

- Top 100 markets simulcasting on digital channels.
- Cable TV with 750 MHz of total bandwidth and Satellite providers must carry 5 or more digital channels with 50% of prime time schedule in digital.

APRIL 2003

50% of analog programming is simulcast on digital channel.

APRIL 2004

75% of analog programming is simulcast on digital channel.

JULY 2004

50% of TV's 36 inches and larger must be HDTV.

APRIL 2005

100% of analog programming is simulcast on digital channel.

JULY 2005

100% of TVs 36 inches and larger and
50% of TVs 25 - 36 inches must be HDTV.

JULY 2006

100% of TVs 25 to 36 inches must be HDTV.

JANUARY 2007

PROPOSED
NTSC signal turn off date.

JULY 2007

100% of all TVs 13 inches and larger must be hdtv and

100% of components with a TV receiver (VCRs, DVR/PVRs etc. to include DTV tuners).

Section 2: How a Television works
The Differences Between Analog TVs & Digital or HDTVs

To best understand how HDTV works, how to choose one, and how to put it all together, you should also learn how analog TVs work. This comparison will help you to understand the meanings of the new HDTV terms.

HOW MOVING PICTURES WORK

A flip book is a simple illustration of how moving pictures work. In the theater, movies show 24 frames per second. Television is 30 frames per second (**"fps"**). Our brain does not process what we see that quickly and the flow of pictures creates motion called **"PERSISTENCE OF VISION"**.

How an Analog, Direct-View, Cathode Ray Tube TV Works

That old TV of yours with the picture tube is an NTSC analog TV. Although features have been added to increase the picture quality, it still works on a system that was in consumers' homes in the 1930s.

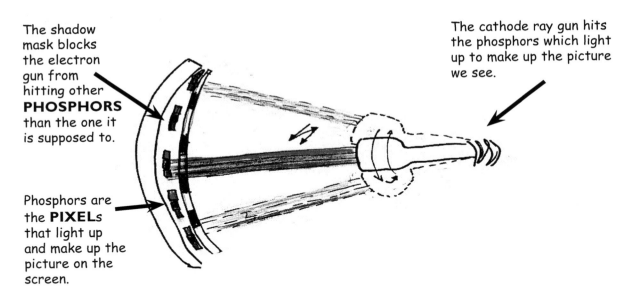

The shadow mask blocks the electron gun from hitting other **PHOSPHORS** than the one it is supposed to.

The cathode ray gun hits the phosphors which light up to make up the picture we see.

Phosphors are the **PIXEL**s that light up and make up the picture on the screen.

TVs and analog broadcasts had limitations. In film each frame is whole and complete like a photograph, unlike a TV signal which has split up each frame into 2 **FIELDS**. (This was originally done in 1941 to keep the picture from fading and rolling). At 1/60th of a second, it is too quick for your brain to perceive and the two fields are **INTERLACED** together in your brain so you perceive a single frame.

1/60 th of a second= 1 "field"

The cathode ray gun scans lines of pixels, the odd lines 1,3, 5, 385 etc. It uses the even lines to set up for the next odd line.

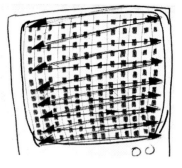

1/60 th of a second= 1 "field"

The cathode ray gun goes back to the top and scans the even lines 2, 4, 424, etc.

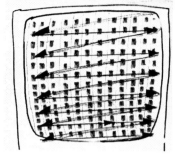

Digital TVs and A Progressive approach ("Progressive Scan," that is)

We know that what makes moving pictures is a series of single pictures (frames) shown in succession (like the flip book). When the frames are divided into 2 fields and interlaced, it was okay on smaller screens. However, on a big screen, a lack of detail, scan lines, and flicker are noticeable. The solution was to show all the lines at once.

PROGRESSIVE SCAN shows a full frame 60 times per second. The result is a more detailed picture without the flickering of an interlaced picture, and for "fixed pixel" displays like LCD TVs, DLP™ TVs or Plasma TVs, there are no scan lines. (This will be further explained later in this chapter).

Progressive scan results in a clearer, more detailed picture. Most new DVD players can output 480p–480 lines of pixels in full frames (the "P" is for progressive scan and "I" is for interlaced). Although this is not High Definition, it will show a superb picture on a digital TV capable of displaying progressive scan. NTSC analog TVs cannot show a progressive scan image.

De-Interlacers and "3:2 Pulldown"

Progressive scan shows a full frame rather than interlaced fields which results in a great quality picture. But a problem exists that many shows are either shot with NTSC interlaced video cameras or film cameras that run at 24 frames per second (and not the 60 fields or 30 frames per second of video). This leads to unclear images and motion **ARTIFACTS** —funny boxes or jagged blurring when objects are moving. By evaluating each field, a **DE-INTERLACER** can determine if the original material was film or video and can make adjustments to fix the problem resulting in the expected great picture quality.

Essentially with de-interlacers and 3:2 pulldown, an equipped TV can correct for loss of picture quality. It is particularly important for programs that were originally film (versus video), like DVDs, movies and some TV shows. The original 24 frames per second must be matched to the 30 frames per second of video through a process called **3:2 PULLDOWN** (or sometimes 2:3 pulldown). De-interlacers use a type of computer chip to evaluate algorithms. You don't have to know how they work. Just know, if you like to watch movies or film shows, you want a TV and/or DVD with a good de-interlacer. (If you do want to know how they work, you can check it out in the Appendix.)

The Resolution Revolution toward a "real life picture"

The whole appeal of HDTV is its clarity—people often refer to it as looking out a window. One way this is achieved is to eliminate scan lines by using progressive scan. The other is to increase the resolution, the number and size of pixels that make up a picture.

You've probably seen a photograph where the picture looked "grainy". You can see the color dots that make up the picture. The result is a picture not as sharp, the color not as bright, and the picture wasn't true to the real subject of the photograph. Although the technology is different with a video signal and your TV, the effect is similar when you have a low resolution picture.

Rocks & mountains are blurry, lack detail.

HIGH RESOLUTION

Picture has a "looking out a window" reality

In video, resolution is determined by the horizontal and vertical scan lines. Each scan line is made up of lines of dots—picture elements or **PIXELS**. As your picture is scanned (or shot onto your picture tube), the higher the number lines, the clearer, brighter and more real the picture becomes.

When the standard for television was set in 1938, with analog signals, the best resolution you could hope for was 330 lines of resolution because this was the most that the RF (radio frequency) signals could carry. (See "Analog and Digital Transmissions" earlier in this chapter.) Some NTSC TVs claim to have "700 lines of resolution". (This does not refer to the resolution that determines HDTV because it is referring to the number of vertical lines. The number of *horizontal lines* is what determines the type of digital TV --480, 720, or 1080.) NTSC TVs can produce only about 200,000 total pixels (dots on the screen).

Over time, new sources increased the lines of resolution fed to the TV. Picture quality began to improve. High 8 video camcorders and Super VHS video recorders upped the ante by creating a signal that carried up to 425 lines of resolution. Along with the higher resolution came stereo HI-FI (high fidelity) sound. Only trouble is, those RF cables could only carry 330 lines of resolution and couldn't carry stereo sound signals.

Enter the RCA or "composite" cables. The video could carry the higher resolution and now there were separate right and left audio cables to carry the stereo sound. Later, a basic surround sound format called **DOLBY PRO-LOGIC®** could be added and sent through those stereo connections as well.

Along came the digital revolution! Digital broadcast satellites, digital Cable TV, and DVDs could now send out almost 500 lines of resolution (nearly twice that of the original signals). That's why you may have heard that these digital sources give you a better picture quality than your old VCR or regular Cable TV. These sources have added digital sound to their increased picture quality allowing for 5.1 discrete (separate) channel **DOLBY DIGITAL®** and **DTS®** surround sound . Audio cables and connections came about to allow the digital sound signal to be sent to the amplifier/receiver.

Then came the *high definition resolution revolution*! A high definition digital signal can come in at as many as 1080 lines of horizontal resolution! —The number of lines counted across the screen from top to bottom. That's **3 times more than your basic Cable TV.** This could produce an image with about 2 million pixels (dots on the screen). That's a total of 10 times more dots than an analog set showing a digital signal!

The result is "looking through a window" reality of color, focus and more—so much so that traditional TV makeup used on actors had to be changed . Now painted backdrops came into focus revealing that a painted library of books had to made of actual books.

NTSC –ANALOG TV

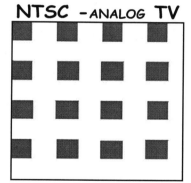

Analog TVs have about 200,000 total pixels. A 40 inch TV will have about 5,000 pixels per square inch.

ATSC-HDTV

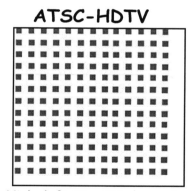

High definition TVs have about 2 million total pixels. A 40 inch TV will have about 50,000 pixels per square inch.

As you can see, the pixels on an analog TV are larger. Therefore, the image is not as sharp and the individual pixels and scan lines become visible by comparison

LINE DOUBLERS/SCALERS

(OR, NOW THAT YOU'VE SEEN HIGH
DEFINITION, HOW CAN YOU WATCH STANDARD
ANALOG NTSC SOURCES?)

Even if you have purchased an HDTV, you may still want to watch some NTSC or standard TV. You may have components like a VCR, or DVD (without progressive scan features) or a PVR/DVR that still have a maximum of 480 interlaced lines or less. These pictures will not have the quality of HDTV signals.

Digital TVs and some analog HDTVs or set top boxes can **UPCONVERT** the signals to give you a better picture quality. This is commonly done by line doubling. Unlike the name implies, **LINE DOUBLERS** do not double the actual scan lines. Instead they typically work by holding the picture for two fields (two 1/2 frames) which creates what appears to be a clearer, brighter picture and eliminates many of the jagged edges that occur during a typical interlaced signal.

Upconverters are available as a separate unit if your TV, set top box, or DVD player does not have the feature.

If you look at the stands you will see a curving pattern in the top picture. The bottom picture has a clear clean image of the stands.

Line doublers don't actually double the number of scan lines as the name might imply...
They work by holding the picture for two fields creating a clearer, brighter picture.

Section 3: Digital TV and HDTV Format

You need to know that **not all digital TVs are capable of showing a high definition picture.** And that **not all broadcasters with digital stations are transmitting high definition**. There are 18 different accepted formats that fit into the following broader formats. Below is a list of the most popular formats and which are considered high definition.

Some LCDs and Plasma TVs have come out with less pixels than is required to show true High Definition. These TVs are considered EDTV. Though they will have a good picture, there was a reason you got such a good deal on that TV. If that is what you want, check that it has the number of scan lines listed in the formats chart for HDTV

As you'll notice, the 2nd number will tell you what kind of digital TV you are looking at—480, 720 or 1080 lines of resolution for SDTV, EDTV, or HDTV.

TYPE OF DIGITAL TV (DEFINITION)	ACTIVE LINES (RESOLUTION)	ASPECT RATIO (SHAPE OF TV)	NOTES
SDTV "Standard Definition" "480i"	640 x 480	4:3 Traditional "Square"	This is the typical NTSC type TV. All TVs that can be hooked up through an analog connection to an HDTV tuner can actually receive the digital stations. However, it will not be a high definition signal and would only show marginal improvement. (Plus HDTV set top boxes can still be costly.)
EDTV "Enhanced Definition" "480p"	704 x 480 ("480 p")	4:3 or 16:9 (widescreen)	Enhanced is 480p, a better picture than NTSC TVs. Many DVD players are EDTV resolution capable.
HDTV "720p"	1280 x 720	16:9	This progressive scan format is best for sports. Some broadcasters use this format.
HDTV "1080i"	1920 x 1080	16:9	Common format for HD broadcast and TVs. Exceptional beauty in still shots.
HDTV "1080p"	1920 x 1080	16:9	Plasma, LCD, and other micropixel screens are native progressive scan because they have no scan lines. This is the best of HDTV today. Some call it "true HDTV". Current broadcast signals must be converted to 1080p. Newer broadcasts will use technologies to handle the increased information required for a 1080p signal.

What's the deal with the different formats and why don't they only show it all as HDTV?

Economic Possibilities of ATSC-Multiple Channels

We've covered history and politics now we can move on to Economics...
Each broadcaster has been allotted their digital bandwidth. They can use it or divide it anyway they please. (See Section 1 of this chapter for bandwidth illustration).

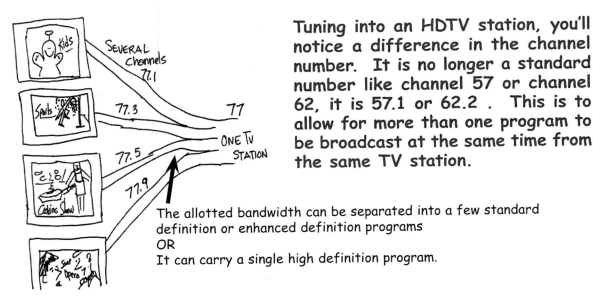

Several channels 77.1

77.3

77.5

77.9

77

ONE TV STATION

Tuning into an HDTV station, you'll notice a difference in the channel number. It is no longer a standard number like channel 57 or channel 62, it is 57.1 or 62.2 . This is to allow for more than one program to be broadcast at the same time from the same TV station.

The allotted bandwidth can be separated into a few standard definition or enhanced definition programs
OR
It can carry a single high definition program.

The bandwidth can handle **one** *High Definition program with digital surround sound* OR it can handle **multiple programs** *in Standard or Enhanced Definition* (because it is not sending as much picture and sound information as a high definition program).

A broadcaster that is sending out more than one digital program on their bandwidth at the same time is said to be **MULTICASTING**.

Multicasting allows a broadcaster to send out different programs in the same time slot. What does that look like? One sub-channel may have just news broadcast in SDTV, another may have children's programming, another a soap opera, etc. Think of the advertising potential for the TV station during one time slot, and you can see why it's a matter of economics.

Already some local broadcasters have opted for this multicasting format. The FCC is working on mandates that will require a percentage of prime-time programming to be broadcast in the HDTV format to ensure that viewers get the full high definition experience. The daytime programming may be multicast with certain programs coming in high definition.

Section 4: HDTV Televisions & Displays

The first thing you will notice is that many HDTVs are shaped differently than your old NTSC TV. That is, they are wider and shorter rather than square. The shape is described in an "**ASPECT RATIO**." You will see terms like "**HD READY**" and "HDTV" . You must understand these terms to know what accessories, benefits and limitations you will encounter from each type of TV.

To be considered an HDTV, it must be capable of displaying an HD format. That is it must be able to show 720 progressive lines or 1080 interlaced lines of resolution. (See previous chart.) Most HDTVs or HD ready TVs can show a progressive scan picture from stations that broadcast 720p or from defines the resolution required for each definition.

The Shape of HDTV: aspect ratio

High Definition formats
are 16:9 aspect ratio,
a wide and shorter
screen. Traditional
NTSC broadcasts are
4:3, almost square.

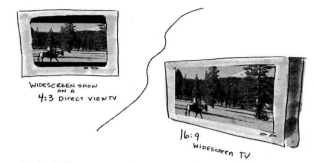

WIDESCREEN SHOW
ON A
4:3 DIRECT VIEW TV

16:9
WIDESCREEN TV

Some high definition ready sets are 4:3 and show the
widescreen 16:9 image with bars on top and bottom.

HDTV (integrated tuner) vs. "HD Ready" TV sets

Some TVs are HDTVs and have built-in or **INTEGRATED TUNERS**. They are ready to be hooked up
to an antenna (or with "**DCR**," to Cable TV) when you take them home. These TVs can show high definition ATSC signals and NTSC analog signals. (See "The Tuner" in chapter 1.)

Other TVs are "**HD READY**". These TVs require an additional tuner from either a set top box or a HD
Satellite or HD Cable TV box. Some HDTVs will come with an added feature called a "**CABLECARD**". These
TVs are also called "**DIGITAL CABLE READY**" or "DCR". The card decodes premium station signals in
the same way a Cable TV box has in the past, receiving your channel subscription information and allowing
you to watch the stations in your monthly plan. (See "Into your Home and to your TV" in Chapter 1).

SET TOP BOX
USES ITS TUNER
TO CHANGE CHANNELS

An HD ready TV requires a set top box ("HD
receiver" or "HD tuner") which will tune into
the channels then feeds the signal to the TV.
(It may be converted to analog before being
sent out or it may send digital signal through a
digital connection depending on the kind of TV.)

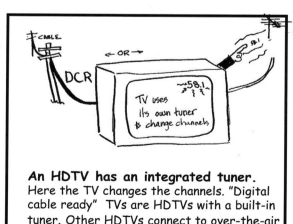

CABLE

← OR →

DCR

TV uses
its own tuner
to change channels

An HDTV has an integrated tuner.
Here the TV changes the channels. "Digital
cable ready" TVs are HDTVs with a built-in
tuner. Other HDTVs connect to over-the-air
antennas.

Section 5: Choosing your HDTV

Now that you know some of the features to look for when buying your HDTV, you find yourself with a choice of many different types of TVs. Just a few years ago your choice was limited to Direct View CRT traditional TVs or rear projection big screens.

Computer technology has given us many new options. LCD, Plasma (or "PDP"), DLP™ TVs , projection, flat panel. What does it all mean and what's the difference? How do they work and how does that affect the quality of the picture? Which one is for you?

We'll begin here by describing each type of HDTV, how they work and how that effects the quality of the picture you will receive. At the end of this section, you'll find a chart comparing the benefits, limitations and buying recommendations for each type of HDTV.

When it comes to HDTV, don't make the common mistake of thinking *all* HDTVs are big screens, though the invention of big screens was the seed of desire for wanting a picture with more detail. As you have seen, by 2007, the FCC has mandated that ALL TVs over 13" (that's small!) will be capable of showing HDTV.

CRTs - "Cathode Ray Tubes"

DIRECT VIEW picture tube TVs and traditional **REAR SCREEN PROJECTION** work with CRT technology. TVs have been CRTs since their invention. Direct View TVs have glass vacuum picture tubes and are often referred to as "traditional TVs" because it is the technology we've known through the history of TV. When "rear projection" big screens were invented, they worked on the same CRT principles.

DIRECT VIEW PICTURE TUBES

Direct View HDTVs can be 4:3 (square) or widescreen 16:9.

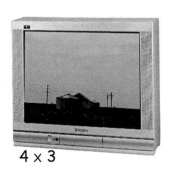

4 x 3

16 x 9

How a CRT works and How it affects picture quality

In section 2 of this chapter, it describes how a CRT works, scanning 60 fields per second, creating an interlaced picture. and that progressive scan will give you more detail than an interlaced picture.

Because a CRT scans lines of phosphors, scan lines can become visible and obvious degrading picture quality. Interlacing can create a blurry picture so be sure that your Direct View HDTV has a de-interlacer and 3:2 pulldown (as described previously). The picture tube, however, is capable of creating dark blacks and good contrast which means that all colors are rich and vibrant. At a distance, pixels and scan lines disappear and you'll want to purchase a TV that is a good size for viewing in your room.

Because of the high cost of manufacturing the picture tubes, and the challenge of making larger vacuum picture tubes, most Direct View TVs are 36 inches or smaller.

High Definition Direct View TVs now come in both traditional 4:3 or widescreen 16:9.

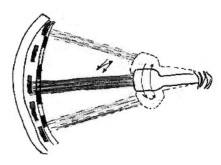

A CRT scans lines of pixels (phosphors) which are lit up to create the picture. It can either interlace the picture or show it progressive scan (See earlier in this chapter).

CRT REAR PROJECTION TVs ("RPTV")

Remember the first big screen in the early 1980s? The picture wasn't very clear. The 480 NTSC scan lines were so spread out on a 48 inch square screen that the picture was jagged and blurry. Today's big screens have 1080 lines with smaller pixels and the result is a smoother, clearer, more detailed picture. For NTSC signals, line doublers and progressive scan have helped to clear up analog signals which is important on a large, rear projection TV. RPTV uses analog, CRT technology. Unlike Direct View CRTs which have a single cathode ray gun, rear projection TVs use 3 guns: red, green, blue.

LCD projection TVs AND DLP™ Projection TVs may look similar in size and shape to RPTVs but they are very different as you will see in the following sections.

Rear projection TVs have deeper cabinets than other big screens because the CRTs must reflect off a mirror to the screen.

HOW A CRT REAR PROJECTION TV ("RPTV") WORKS AND HOW IT AFFECTS PICTURE QUALITY:

Three beams (red, green and blue) scan the picture onto a mirror at the back of the TV that reflects back through the material that makes up the front screen.

The front screen has ridges that amplify the light of the image as it comes through for you to see (called a **LENTICULAR SCREEN**) These screens are delicate and it is best to get a screen protector if you live with kids, pets or rambunctious friends.

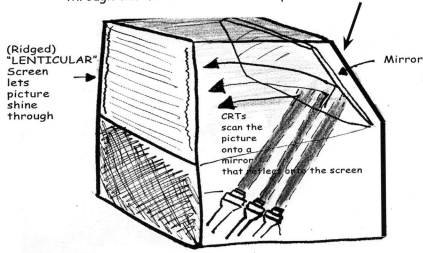

(Ridged) "LENTICULAR" Screen lets picture shine through

Mirror

CRTs scan the picture onto a mirror that reflects onto the screen

Not all projection big screens are RPTVs. RPTV refer to picture images reflected off of a mirror onto the screen. Other projection TVs, like LCDs send the image directly to the screen.

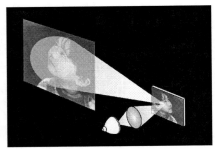

Rear projection TVs are **"reflective"** use a mirror to project the image.

Photos courtesy of Royal Philips

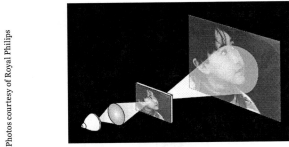

"TRANSMISSIVE" projection TVs send light through a panel that magnifies the image and projects it directly onto the screen.

CARE OF REAR PROJECTION TVs

RPTVs have a couple of unique requirements for care and maintenance that you will not find on other big screens. One consideration is that the lenticular screen, which is the front screen of the TV, is delicate and can be scratched or torn by pets, rambunctious kids, or other household accidents. You will want to be sure that your TV comes with (or you can purchase) a screen cover. Next, the 3 CRTs need to be regularly re-aligned, preferably by a professional. (You probably won't notice that the picture has degraded just as we don't notice how our kids grow every day.) And finally, rear projection TVs and plasma TVs share the problem of "burn-in" of static images. Be aware of the needs of your TV to ensure a quality, problem free picture.

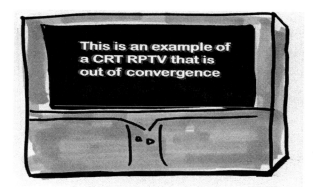

CONVERGENCE:

ALIGNING THE CRTs

The three light beams can slowly become out of sync and not combine on the precise pixels. Red or blue outlines of objects (especially noticeable on words) can result in a blurry picture. The act of lining up the 3 lights is called convergence. Some TVs claim to have auto convergence, most benefit from doing it manually.

You can bring in a professional who can optimize your picture with the use of special meters . (**ISF CERTIFIED**). For best results have your TV tuned up every 6 months so that it will continue to have a showroom quality picture.

BURN-IN

RPTVs and Plasma TVs are sensitive to static pictures left on screen. A phosphor that is lit consistently for a long period of time will retain that color and intensity. You should never leave a desktop computer screen, nor play video games with a static background, nor leave any static picture, like a DVD menu or a photograph on the screen for long periods of time. Even black bars on 4:3 transmitted pictures or narrow widescreen movies, or running stock price or news banners can have bad effects if left onscreen for extended periods of time. This is called "**BURN-IN**" and will leave a ghost image of the static information on your screen that will be super-imposed over whatever you watch from then on.

"Fixed Pixel" Displays

Digital displays have advantages over analog displays. While an analog display relies on an image scanned horizontally across the screen, creating lines, flicker, and jagged edges, digital displays allot a separate picture element, with its own information, for each pixel on the screen. With each frame, a pixel lights up in the intensity and color that it receives from the digital signal information. This also means that **FIXED PIXEL** TVs are built as progressive scan displays. This is often referred to as "native 720p" or "native 1080p" meaning that's the way they naturally show the picture. Some "fixed pixel" displays are created by the pixels being projected onto the screen, others are flat panels that display the pixels.

DLP™ TVs are a type of "fixed pixel" display where each pixel is individually projected. They are progressive scan (there are no scan lines). They can create bright, clear pictures.

photos courtesy of
RCA, A Thomson Brand

DLP TVs (aka DMD or Micropixel displays)

DLP™ chips are also referred to as **DIGITAL LIGHT PROCESSING™** and have also been called **DMD** or **DIGITAL MICROMIRROR DEVICES.** They produce a very bright image. The size of these TVs are narrower and lighter than similar RPTV screen sizes. Some can even be hung on the wall.

Because a DLP™ TV is progressive scan, you will not see scan lines as you do on an RPTV and because it projects the image through a color wheel, there is no problem with "burn-in". Care and maintenance is minimal. DLP™ displays will usually cost more than a traditional CRT rear projection TV, yet less than other fixed pixel displays like a flat screen plasma.

How a DLP™ TV (DMD) works and How it affects picture quality
(This is really cool technology!)

On a small chip (that can fit in the palm of your hand), there is a million microscopic mirrors that tilt into an "on" or "off" position. Each reflects light from a light bulb through a color wheel. The direction and angle of the tilt creates the color and intensity of each pixel on the screen. All the pixels work together to create the picture projected onto your TV screen.

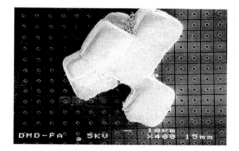

A microscopic image of the mirrors on the chip that creates the picture as compared to a grain of salt!

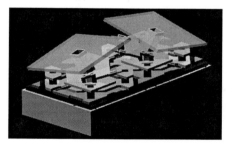

Each mirror angle corresponds to a single pixel and reflects light through the color wheel that will make up the picture on the screen.

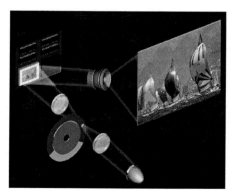

Illustrations courtesy of Texas Instruments

A DLP™ TV uses a color wheel to create the colors instead of separate colored light beams. It uses a simple household light bulb to project the image. The bulb is housed in an easy access area where you can change it when the bulb burns out. Because it is one light beam, there is no convergence.

DLP™ projection TVs are often about 17 inches deep.

This Thomson RCA DLP™ projection TV is narrower than this book width and light enough to be hung on the wall, thus rivaling a flat screen Plasma or LCD TV.

LCDs: Liquid Crystal Displays — Rear Projection and Flat Panels
(aka "LCTV" or "Liquid Crystal Television")

Liquid Crystal has been around a long time. Today's TV technology has its roots in the LCDs used in calculator or digital watch displays. Of course the current **LIQUID CRYSTAL DISPLAY**s have become more sophisticated and are capable of showing a beautiful, detailed color picture. There are two types of LCD TVs. The LCD flat panel creates the picture directly to the screen. The second type of LCD uses a projection technology. Light is transmitted through a small LCD panel and projected onto the screen. Naturally, flat panel LCDs have better contrast and richer colors than the LCD projection TVs. At this time, most LCD flat panels are 46 inch screens or smaller because they will become cost prohibitive for most of us in larger sizes.

photo courtesy of Sharp Electronics Corp.
Photographer: Jason Ware

LCD Projection TV

Photo courtesy of Sony Electronics

HOW LCDs WORK AND HOW IT AFFECTS PICTURE QUALITY

When the LCD TV receives a signal, picture element (pixel) information is given to electrodes which, based on variations in voltage, twist and straighten the liquid crystal. The shape of the crystal determines how much light can pass through. A straight crystal, like a closed blind creates dark colors.

The liquid crystals are sandwiched between polarized glass panels, one vertically polarized, one horizontally, which, combined with the twisted crystal determines how much light gets through. The light is then sent through a color filter to create its individual picture element, which together with its 2 million fellow pixels create the picture on your screen.

One traditional limitation of LCD TVs has been the response time, the time it takes for the crystal to twist. While this time is imperceptible to viewers, the result is motion ghosting that looks like ghosting trails. This is particularly noticeable on fast-motion sports programming. However, many of the higher-quality LCD panels from leading manufacturers no longer have this issue. These newer panels also eliminate the poor viewing angles formerly associated with LCD TVs, as they boast a minimum of 170 degrees both horizontally and vertically, as well as extremely high brightness and low glare reflection.

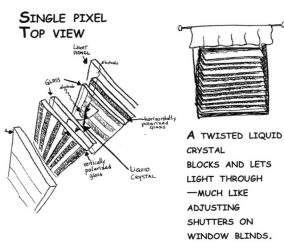

SINGLE PIXEL
TOP VIEW

A TWISTED LIQUID CRYSTAL BLOCKS AND LETS LIGHT THROUGH —MUCH LIKE ADJUSTING SHUTTERS ON WINDOW BLINDS.

Plasma Displays ("PDP")
(THAT ALLURING, HANG-ON-THE-WALL FLAT SCREEN TV!)

photo courtesy LG Electronics

PLASMA is the buzz word in HDTV. So many people love the idea of a large TV that takes up little space in the living room and are known for outstanding picture quality. When they first came on the market, quality control and manufacturing capabilities made them exorbitant in price, but with practice and time, they are becoming more affordable. Pay attention to the resolution listed for the Plasma Display as manufacturers offer EDTV displays with only 480 lines of resolution that are not true High Definition. If you are trying to save money and are sitting a distance from the screen, this may be a good option to fit a Plasma TV into your budget. Let your eyes be your guide.

HOW A PLASMA DISPLAY WORKS AND HOW IT AFFECTS PICTURE QUALITY

"Plasma" refers to the gas that fills the cells that make up each picture element (pixel). It helps to think of plasma working similar to a neon sign. The picture information is fed to electrodes for each pixel on the screen containing instructions for varying the voltage and intensity of charge on the gas. The voltage will create the proper combination of colors and intensity for that pixel, the gas emits an ultraviolet light which activates the phosphor on the screen and along with its 2 million fellow phosphors make up the picture on your screen. The direct, onscreen light created by each gas-filled pixel chamber is the key to the Plasma's superior picture quality. There are no scan lines or interlacing to see flicker. The light does not have to come through layers like an LCD, so the picture is generally brighter and more vibrant, and does not have the viewing angle problems of an LCD or RPTV. Also, unlike LCD TVs that are twisting liquid crystals, there is a direct response to information for each pixel, so a plasma is better suited for motion like in action movies or sports. One limitation of the phosphor technology, like RPTVs, there is the risk of "burn-in" (see "care and maintenance of RPTVs"). Newer models may have technology which will reduce this risk. Check specifications for features like "pixel orbiting" if you want to play video games, use the Plasma as a computer display, or you will need to zoom in any picture that doesn't fill the screen.

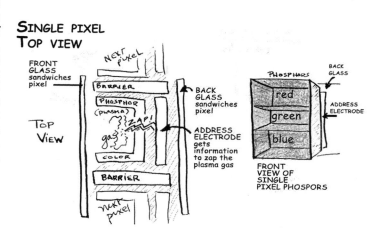

SINGLE PIXEL TOP VIEW

FRONT GLASS sandwiches pixel

NEXT pixel

BARRIER

PHOSPHOR (PLASMA)

TOP View

gas

ZAP!

COLOR

BARRIER

next pixel

BACK GLASS sandwiches pixel

ADDRESS ELECTRODE gets information to zap the plasma gas

PHOSPHORS

BACK GLASS

red

green

blue

ADDRESS ELECTRODE

FRONT VIEW OF SINGLE PIXEL PHOSPORS

"LCoS" Liquid Crystal On Silicon

LCoS works much like LCDs. This technology has become viable after a rocky start where it was taken off the market for buzzing problems in rooms with fluorescent lights.   LCos is used in both front and rear projection TV systems. Because the LCoS technology is reshaping as fast as its liquid crystals that make up the picture, it is only covered in summary... Like LCD, three color panels red, green and blue, are combined to get a full color image. The liquid crystal is twisted and shaped by a transistor as it is in LCD; however, the transistor is on the other side of the crystal so it doesn't get in the way of the light shined onto the liquid crystal. This means a brighter picture, less contrast, wider viewing angles and more vibrant colors than an LCD. Typically with LCos, there is less space between each pixel which creates more detail. The technology it takes to make this work is precise and you will pay a premium for this great image.

New Liquid Crystal Technologies

Liquid crystal can be used in other ways to create stunning images. How the light shines through panels, and/or reflects off mirrors, and how many plates are used, can improve the picture quality. Sony is one company that has again created an innovative display technology that creates stunning picture. The SXRD™ or "Silicon Xtal Reflective Display", creates a full 1920 x 1080 pixel picture which is true high definition at its best. Sony has created its microdisplay with a higher number of pixels and smaller gaps between pixels to create stunningly clear and true to life pictures. They also use a unique system of transmitted and reflecting light. What you want to know is that the image is created on a small chip inside the TV that is projected onto the screen of the TV.

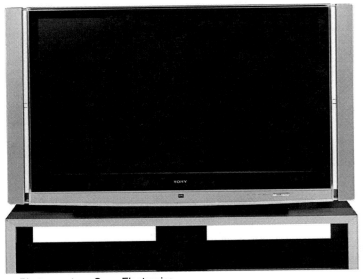

Photo courtesy Sony Electronics

Projectors- aka "Front Projection TVs"

Front projectors shine their image onto a screen much like the movie screens we used to watch home movies (technology, of course, has made them capable of much better picture quality).

photo courtesy of Yamaha

The **FIRST PROJECTION TV**s were 3 CRT beams projected in red green and blue and were the size of a coffee table set in the middle of a darkened room (similar to a movie theater). The projectors are much smaller today. Now, with the use of 3 chip DLPs, and LCoS, projectors have gotten brighter, clearer, able to be seen in brightly lit rooms. These projectors are also quieter and able to be hung from the ceiling or hidden in ceiling panels or other furniture.

Because there is no danger of ghost imaging, they are good for use with computers, video games and other static images. The screens can be 120 inch diagonally providing a real theater experience.

Buying a projector like this means someone in your household is into the home theater experience. Although your room doesn't have to be fully dark like a movie theater, colors are rich and vibrant in a darkened room, and you will want to be sure light does not fall directly on the screen. You will usually want to have a projector professionally installed as you may have in wall or ceiling wires to run.

The thing to remember if you are a bystander watching your loved one choose a front projection TV is that it isn't a movie projector, it's still a TV. Controlling and hookups will be often the same as if the image was just coming to you out of a TV screen.

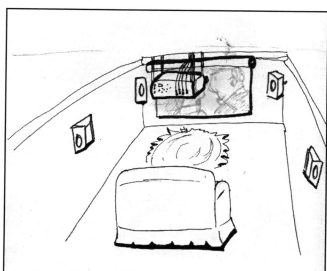

You will probably want to arrange your room to view the projection TV optimally. Though today's projection TVs can be viewed in brighter light, you will not want direct light on the screen, and may opt for a darkened room to optimize the depth of color and picture.

HDTV COMPARISON

TYPE OF TV	BEST FOR...	A QUALITY SET WILL ADDRESS...	COST	IMPORTANT NOTES..
CRT Direct View	NTSC programs, small rooms, budget. *Gorgeous picture from a distance.*	Close up, scan lines obvious can have jagged or blurry picture	Many are under $1,000, more features and 16:9 cost more	Get a model with de-interlacing, and 3:2 pulldown for best picture.
CRT Rear Projection TV	Good budget choice for big screen	Large cabinet, limited viewing angle, scan lines and pixels visible.	Can get over 46 inch for under $1,000. Many under $2,000.	NTSC can look terrible without line doublers, de-interlacers and 3:2 pulldown.
DLP™ TV (Projection)	**Sports**. Bigger screens for less than LCD or Plasma. Good contrast. and black No burn-in	May lack detail and clarity you could find in flat panel.	Similar to LCD projection. 52 inch available under $3,000; 56 inch and above is $3,000 to $4,000.	This is an excellent choice for a bigger screen size. Very good viewing angle for side viewing.
LCD Projection	**Movies.** Big screen at good price.	Lower quality is best viewed straight on, picture fades from side or off eye-level. Look for black level and color intensity. Response time can cause ghosts in fast movements like sports.	See DLP™ TV, prices are comparable.	Look for models that address motion issues and viewing angles. Use what you like as a guide. Contrast ratios are not measured the same as plasma.
LCoS	**Beautiful movies.** Better blacks, color and detail. than LCDs. Better viewing angles than LCD. Similar quality to DLP™ TV.	Had problems in past with fluorescent lighting and other difficulties. Worked out in newer TVs that don't use term "LCoS"	Anywhere from $2500 to $5,000 or more depending on the brand and exact technology.	May come with other names, check product descriptions to see if new technology is LCoS.
LCD Flat Panel	**Video Games, computer.** Smaller screens great for kitchens and other rooms. Lightweight and thin--great to hang on wall. Energy Efficient.	Loses a little picture quality from side viewing. Over 46" is costly. ***May not perform as well as plasma in brightly lit rooms.***		Picture quality is much better than LCD projection. No burn-in.
Plasma - Flat Panel	**Sports, Movies, TV Programming. Bright rooms.** Great color and detail. Handles motion well.	Older models prone to burn-in. Limited pixel life. (okay about 10 years of constant viewing!) May make buzzing noise in mountain areas over 6500 feet.	If it's under $2,000 and over 42 inches, it is probably EDTV or interlaced. 42" can start around $3,000.	If you watch TV more than 6 hours every day, it may last only 10 years, look for longer life plasma. EDTV and interlaced plasmas may not give you picture quality as good as some other choices for the same price.
Front projection	**Home Theater Experience. Sports.** Huge picture.	May not be suitable for rooms with bright lighting.		Recommend professional installation for in wall wiring.

Section 6 : HDTV Audio Format AC-3
Digital Audio Surround Sound vs... Analog Surround Sound

In HDTV, along with great picture comes great sound. By seeing how Digital Surround Sound differs from other sound options, you can decide if you want to take advantage of it. Choosing home theater surround options also will affect your choices on how to hook up and run your system.

History of TV sound

In the beginning...
There was one speaker ("mono"). The antenna was hooked up with a single cable that carried picture and was limited to mono sound.

With the invention of RCA composite audio cables, the signal could be split into left and right, that is, "stereo" (Video had a separate cable.)

As technology progressed, audio receivers/amplifiers with stereo sound could be "matrixed" into more speakers Recording engineers put a code in the stereo signal that split the sound to fill the room starting with 4 speaker "quadraphonic". When *Star Wars* came into theaters, the filmmakers created sound that would surround the viewers and make them feel more part of the action. Home theater brought this idea into our homes.

This matrixed analog sound was brought to us by Dolby™ Laboratories (who had been cleaning up our cassette music with Dolby Noise Reduction™).   It is called "Dolby Pro-Logic™" or often just "surround sound". The sound is separated into 5 channels to go to 5 speakers. A front left and a front right speaker that have different information (like stereo), play music and sound effects. A center channel speaker plays the voice or dialog, and two surround speakers act together playing ambient sounds that appear to come from behind. Surround sound uses 5.1 speakers. The ".1" refers to the subwoofer or bass speaker, which because it carries only low frequencies effects ("LFE") is referred to as .1 channel (the poor subwoofer doesn't get full speaker status since it doesn't carry a full audio signal range.)

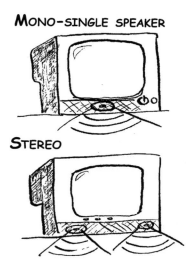

MONO–SINGLE SPEAKER

STEREO

5.1 SURROUND SOUND

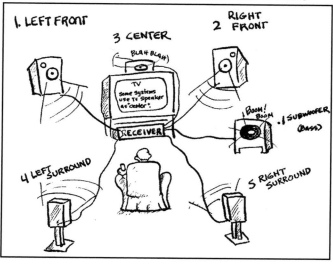

1. LEFT FRONT

3 CENTER

BLAH BLAH)

TV
Some systems use TV speaker as center".

RECEIVER

RIGHT 2 FRONT

BOOM! BOOM .1 SUBWOOFER (BASS)

4 LEFT SURROUND

5 RIGHT SURROUND

SURROUND SOUND OR "DOLBY PRO LOGIC®" OR DTS™ NEO 6

With basic Dolby® surround or "Pro Logic"® or DTS:Neo™ a sound like an airplane, can pass from FRONT TO BACK as if it were going overhead.

Because basic surround sound sends out an analog signal, it is matrixed. This means that the surround speakers get their information from a code in the stereo signal. The sound gives you a feeling of being "surrounded" but there is no direction to the sound from the back speakers. (See Connections Chapter "How you get surround sound from a stereo connection.")

With the ability to transmit digital sound signals, information could be sent to each individual speaker (referred to as **"DISCRETE" CHANNELS**). It must be sent to a Dolby Digital® or DTS® Receiver which can decode the information. The rear speakers could have separate information and now a bullet could ricochet to every corner of the room. A helicopter could circle you. Someone could sneak in to the door behind your right shoulder, while a baby cried over your left shoulder. You are now in the middle of the action!

Note: and they don't stop with 5.1, there is now 6.1, 7.1, 8. (Each adds more surround speakers to further put you in the middle of the action. DTS™-ES™ and Dolby Digital™ 7.1 create the information for the other speakers. Where will it end?

AC-3 --DOLBY DIGITAL, DTS™

EACH SPEAKER GETS ITS OWN DISCRETE INFORMATION.

With Dolby Digital™ surround, each speaker gets its own "discrete" sound information. A helicopter can pass in a circle around you coming out of each speaker separately left front to right front to right rear to left rear and around...as if circling the room.

High Definition TV sends digital sound signals that allows for discrete separate signals, "channels", to be sent to each of 5 speakers (expanding to 6 and 7 and 8 speakers) and a low frequency speaker.

You do not need HDTV to enjoy AC-3 Dolby Digital™ or DTS™ surround sound. Digital NTSC signals like DVDs and some Satellite broadcasts have made digital surround available. (You will learn that to receive Digital Surround, you must have a digital audio hookup into a receiver that can convert the digital sound to analog.)

A note about Home Theater audio/video receivers: When Dolby Digital™ and DTS™ first came on the market, DVD players and components had the "decoders" built in. The digital information was decoded in the component and then fed to receiver through 6 analog cables so that it could amplify the sound and send it to the speakers. As new sound technologies are developed, like music discs encoded with DVD audio or SACD, components are again decoding **SACD** and DVD-Audio information which again, must be sent to the amplifier via analog audio cables. (See Connection and Cable Chapters for 6 channel line audio.) Most a/v receivers now have Dolby Digital™ and DTS™ decoders and can convert the signal from any DVD player therefore they can be connected with a digital connection. A/V receivers are catching up.

Section 7 : What you need to receive HDTV

Today, almost anywhere you live in the United States, you can receive HDTV programming. HDTV is available by over-the-air antenna, high definition Cable TV, or high definition Satellite dish.

TO GET A HIGH DEFINITION PICTURE ON YOUR TV, YOU'LL NEED:

- An HD-ready TV and set top HDTV tuner (may be combined with Cable TV or Satellite box) *or*
- An Integrated HDTV
- Either an Antenna, Satellite or High Definition Cable TV
- A Dolby Digital™ Surround Receiver and 5.1 speakers (Optional).
- Digital video cable connections *or* component video cables (see "connections" and "cables" chapters).

Getting the HDTV signal
(REVIEW "GETTING THE SIGNAL" SECTION OF THE TUNER CHAPTER FOR A BETTER UNDERSTANDING)

By 2006, almost everyone will have the ability to receive at least some HDTV stations, either via off-air, Cable TV or Satellite

If you live in an area where you receive over-the-air signals, you can use a UHF antenna to receive the HDTV stations. The Satellite providers have many premium high definition stations like HDNet, HBO and Showtime in HD, ESPN-HD, Discovery HD, and more. The list is growing monthly. Satellite providers are offering local HD stations first in the larger markets and then rolling out to all households and they offer Network programming, so you may still need an antenna to receive local stations if you live where you receive off-air TV stations.

Cable TV providers are getting on board and by 2006, most will offer an array of premium, and local and Network stations. (See CableCard™)

OVER-THE-AIR ANTENNAS
(AKA: TERRESTRIAL BROADCASTS OR "OTA")

Can you receive an HDTV signal? What kind? How powerful of an antenna do you need? Visit www.antennaweb.org --from the Consumer Electronics Association, fill in you zip and you can find out what kind of antenna you need and which direction to point it.

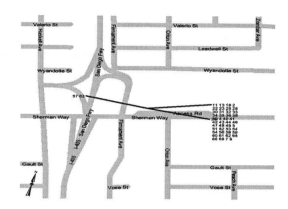

Remember: HDTV signals come in over the UHF spectrum. This means that you need a UHF antenna.

The UHF antenna is the round part of the antenna and not the straight antenna on set top antennas like "rabbit ears".

Antenna pictured here from
Terk Technologies, Inc.

On a rooftop antenna, the arrow part of the antenna receives UHF.

New antennas are available that specialize in HDTV signals. Each will have a color code that you can check with antennaweb to see if it will work for you.

HIGH DEFINITION SATELLITE

Whether you are new to Satellite or are already a Satellite subscriber, you may need a new HD dish. Some are elliptical (oval) to receive both the NTSC stations and to face a second Satellite which sends down High Definition information, and now another Satellite for local TV stations.

Note: If you use a Satellite receiver, you may not need an additional HDTV tuner for your HD ready TV.

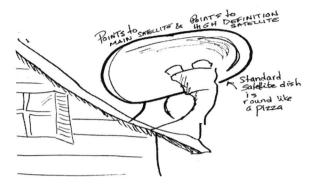

HIGH DEFINITION CABLE TV OPTIONS

High Definition Cable TV may require a set top box or it may utilize a CableCard that is inserted into HDTVs that are "digital cable ready"—"DCR" TVs. CableCards will unscramble premium channels so you can use the tuner in the TV to change channels.

Note: new High Definition Cable TV boxes have HD tuners so you may not need a separate HD tuner for your HD ready TV.

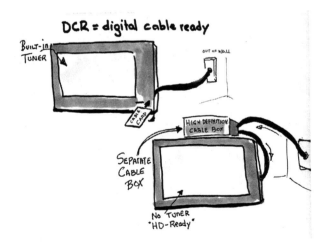

The Ins & Outs of Connections

WHAT YOU WILL LEARN IN CHAPTER 3...

-Where to look for the connections on each piece of equipment.

-How to identify the difference between inputs and outputs.

-How inputs hook up to outputs and how outputs hook up to inputs.

-How to do an inventory for use in your hookup.

-How to identify the different kinds of connections and what difference it will make to chose one over the other.

-How to choose the best connection for your needs.

-How device jacks are grouped to handle a device and labeled as a single input or output.

Words to know in this chapter:

A/V RECEIVER
ASSIGNABLE INPUT
BI-DIRECTIONAL
BITSTREAM
BNC
CHROMA
COAXIAL CABLE
COAXIAL DIGITAL CABLE
COMPONENT VIDEO
COMPOSITE VIDEO
D SUB 15
DIGITAL AUDIO
DIGITAL DECODER
DTV LINK
DVD-AUDIO
DVI
ETHERNET
FIBER OPTIC
FIREWIRE
F-PIN CABLE
HD 15 D-SUB
HDCP
HDMI
HI-FI
HIGH   DEFINITION   MULTIMEDIA
INTERFACE
IEEE1394
ILINK
INPUT
JACK PANEL, "JACK PACK", "INPUT
PANEL"
JACKS
LINE AUDIO
LINE AUDIO
LUMINANCE
MATRIXED SURROUND SOUND
OPTICAL

OUTPUT
PCM
RCA PHONO PLUG CONNECTORS
RF CONNECTION
RGB-HV
RS-232
SACD
SUPER VHS VCR
S-VIDEO
TERMINALS
TOSLINK
USB
VGA
Y/C

SECTION 1: What connections do & how to find them

To send a signal that contains picture and sound (and sometimes other information) from one device to another, there are connections on each piece of your equipment. Hooking up equipment is one of the most frustrating and misunderstood parts of buying, setting up and using your home entertainment components. It makes more sense when you start at the beginning. First, you need to identify the connections available on each component before deciding how you will hook it up.

The ins and outs of terminals

"**TERMINALS**" or "**JACKS**", as device connections are called, are used to send signals from one piece of equipment to another. These are the portals from which and to which information (that is picture and sound) is sent and received. After the source of the picture does its work—it receives a broadcast signal or it reads media like VHS or DVD—it sends the picture and sound out, which is then received by the next component/device. Sometimes that device is the TV, and sometimes it hooks into another component before going on to the TV. A Cable TV or Satellite box may send the information to a VCR or DVR or DVD recorder for you to record and view at a later time. But ultimately the TV will accept and display the picture from all other devices/components.

Whether it is a single jack that accepts both picture and sound, like an RF antenna Cable TV, or HDMI, or a group of separate audio and video jacks for a single component, each grouping is either an "Input" or "Output." The first step in hooking up is identifying the connections on your equipment.

Turn your equipment around and get familiar with the connections.

I feel so exposed!

The source **sends out** its information. It does this **via an OUTPUT** jack. It runs OUT the cable **to the next device** (or TV) which accepts that information **IN** through its **INPUT** jack. That device will then either record it or display it.

Here is an example of how it works:

You may have digital Satellite or Cable TV, or a premium Cable TV channel coming into your house from the wall connection. The signal travels through a cable IN to the Satellite or Cable TV box. The box then does its decoding and/or converting and sends the resulting picture and sound OUT through the cables connected to its output jack. The recorder (VHS, DVD, hard disc recorder), then accepts the picture and sound IN through its INPUT jacks. When you want to play what it has recorded, it will send the picture and sound OUT through the output jacks and IN to the TV through one of the TV's inputs. The recorder can also pass the picture and sound straight through. (See Chapter 1 VCR passthrough.) ("Input"–Have you ever seen that word on a remote control or the back of your TV?) Inputs can also be labeled "video 1, 2, 3 etc."

FLOW OF A CABLE TV OR SATELLITE SIGNAL

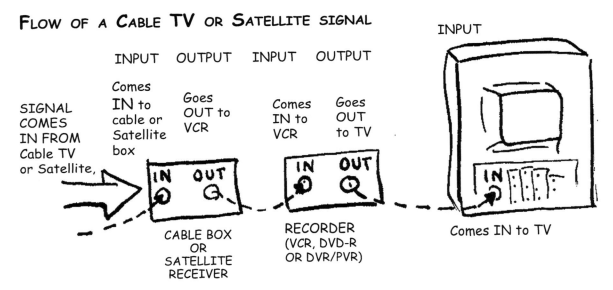

Discovering and identifying connections

You are an EXPLORER. Your job is to identify what you see on your equipment. You will note what types of jacks you discover and what they are named or labeled on your equipment. The Hookup guide form in Chapter 5 will give you a place to note your findings (be sure to read through the directions before you start writing). Record what types of connections you find, how many of each type of input and output you find on each device and how they are labeled on the device. There are real world examples at the end of this chapter. This will give you practice in discovering the terminals and how they might be set up or labeled. The number of inputs a TV or receiver has will determine how you will hook up your equipment.

You don't have to make any choices right now. Just note what you find.

Cables come with different shaped connectors which fit into different shaped terminals. Use this chapter as a reference to recognize the shapes and colors of the connections to identify them.

There are single connectors like RCA phono, f-pin screw on and push on, and the professional screw on "BNC"

DVI, HDMI and other pin type connectors have individual pins or a row of flat pins

Most jacks will be found on the rear panel of your equipment. On some flat panel TVs, there are jacks on the side. Some jacks can be found on ledges and lips surrounding the "**JACK PANEL**". If you find a label and no jack, be sure to look around near the label. On **A/V RECEIVERS** you might find "**ASSIGNABLE.**" This means that although it may be labeled as a "DVD in" (for example), it can be assigned for use with another device.

For the convenience of hooking up a temporary device like a camcorder or video game, some TVs also have jacks on the front or under a spring-loaded door on the front of the TV. Be sure to look everywhere.

Flat panel TVs often have connections on the side so they can lie flat against the wall.

Though you will want to count front jacks, you will probably only use them for devices that you hook up temporarily like a camcorder, video game, digital camera, laptop, etc.

Be sure to look for hidden doors on the front and sides of your TV or other device.

SECTION 2: Identifying the connections on your equipment
Video Connections: what they look like, what they do

antenna connection on
back of TV

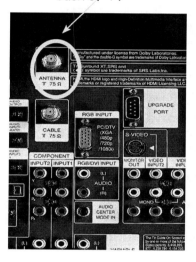

antenna or cable input and
output on DVR

RF CONNECTION
Also called: Coaxial video input, f-pin, "antenna"

The "RF" in this connection is short for "radio frequency". This does *not* mean that it only carries sound or brings in radio stations. Radio frequency refers to the range of frequencies that can carry an analog signal with sound and light waves. It carries both audio and video.

REASON FOR USE:

To bring in the signal from an antenna, Cable TV or Satellite from the wall or as a simple sound and picture hook up between certain component or devices. This connection **does *not* carry stereo HI-FI sound** unless it is bringing in a digital signal from Satellite or digital Cable TV!

HOW TO SPOT THIS CONNECTION:
(WHAT IT LOOKS LIKE)

This is the terminal that is threaded like a screw. The screw-on mount has a small hole in its center (for the "f" pin). A push on f-pin connector can also be used, though the connection is not as secure as screw on connectors. This is the connection that often is labeled "antenna" or even "ant In" or "cable in" or "sat in". It could also be labeled aux (for auxiliary) or "in from cable" or "CATV." On a Satellite, Cable TV or HDTV box, if it is labeled "cable in" or "sat in", be sure that is what you connect (not antenna).

EQUIPMENT ON WHICH YOU MIGHT FIND THIS CONNECTION:

TVs—from the very basic televisions to high end TVs. (All but TVs prior to 1980).

VCRs—there will be both an input and an output jack on VCRs.

Cable TV or Satellite boxes—there will be both an input and an output terminal on these boxes.

You will *not* find this connection on a DVD player. You may wonder, "what if that is the only connection my TV has?" You will need an RF modulator. (See "Accessories" section of the Hook Up Planning and Prep Chapter.)

It is called "Composite" because it combines the black and white and color information that make up the color picture information.

RCA JACKS
Also called: A/V jacks "Audio/Video jacks" or "COMPOSITE" terminals

RCA connections are the most common. Using a single video, and a right and a left audio channel for stereo (older, mono or non-stereo units will have a yellow video and only one audio jack). These jacks got their name because they were invented by RCA laboratories.

REASON FOR USE:
Carries video and audio separately in and out from equipment. This allows for stereo and simple surround sound. It CARRIES ONLY ANALOG SIGNALS. For this reason, you cannot have full Dolby Digital® surround sound with its five discrete channels (see glossary and HDTV chapter 2 for more about digital surround sound).

HOW TO SPOT THIS CONNECTION:
(WHAT IT LOOKS LIKE)
These connections have a hole in the middle of a raised yellow, white or red circle. Usually grouped together, they will be labeled yellow "VIDEO" "AUDIO" white, "L", and red, "R" (for "left" and "right") (easiest to remember that "red' and "right" start with "r".) As a group these connections will be labeled "Input" or "Output" or "Video 1 (2, 3 etc)".

=========SPECIAL BULLETIN==========
There are many connections with the same shape as the RCA connectors. These cables have "phono" type ends that push in to the connections. If they have any colors other than the pairing of yellow and red and white, they may be for another kind of connection. Component video connections, and even some audio connections have the same shape.
Red, green, and blue jacks that are grouped together are component (video only) connections. Or there could be an orange or a black or even a brown connection that is used for a coaxial digital audio cable.
For composite cables we are looking for Yellow video and Red and White audio.
==
Now back to our regularly scheduled program...

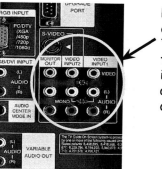

RCA input on TV. There are two video inputs and one output

EQUIPMENT ON WHICH YOU MIGHT FIND THIS CONNECTION:

This is the ubiquitous connection. That is, you see this connection ALMOST EVERYWHERE. As far as video equipment goes, the only place you may NOT find an RCA/composite terminal is on an entry level or older TV set. For some of these televisions, it is possible that there is only a coaxial/antenna/f-pin input.

This is the RCA connection on the back of a DVD player. The video (yellow) is separate from the 2 channel right and left audio. You will use the yellow, red and white outputs to hook into one input on your TV or A/V receiver if you don't have better options.

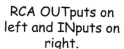

HOW YOU GET SURROUND SOUND FROM A STEREO (A RIGHT AND A LEFT) CONNECTION?

Dolby Pro Logic® and basic surround sound send audio via a **MATRIXED SOUND** format, that is, the information is mixed into the right and left channels. Once it reaches an A/V receiver that has the decoder, it can be heard through 5 speakers surrounding the room.

RCA OUTputs on left and INputs on right.

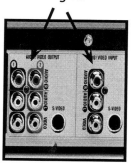

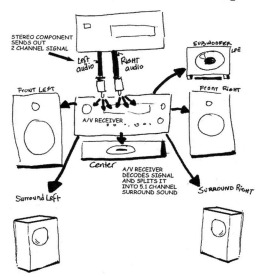

(See HDTV Chapter 2, section 6: HDTV Audio Format for more about Dolby Pro Logic® and Dolby Digital® surround sound.)

S-video input on TV. The line shows that the S-video can be used with video input 2

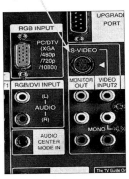

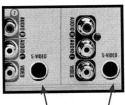

S-Video output (on left) and S-Video input (on right) can "pass-through" the S-Video signal.

S-VIDEO
Also called: "Y/C" connector
and sometimes "S-VHS"

This jack is used only for video signal. It is often used along with audio RCA cables. Alternatively, it can be paired with a digital audio connection. The pins in the cable's connector fit into a set of holes in the S-Video terminal.

REASON FOR USE
The S-Video jack is used to achieve a higher quality picture. It can separate the "**CHROMA**" which is the color information, from the brightness—called **LUMINANCE** (think "illuminate"). The "y" stands for the luminance and the "C" is for chroma. This will give a brighter picture with a larger array of distinct colors. It can also eliminate shimmer.

TV stations send out the broadcast with the chroma and luminance separated. Analog televisions must separate the chroma and luminance to display the picture. While RF cables and RCA video cables combine the signal, S-video keeps the signal separate allowing for less processing and less chance of distorting the picture.

HOW TO SPOT THIS CONNECTION:
(WHAT IT LOOKS LIKE)

The S-Video or "y/c" connection is a female jack --like most on your equipment. It is round and black with holes in a particular pattern as illustrated.

EQUIPMENT ON WHICH YOU MIGHT FIND THIS CONNECTION:

Because of its better quality picture, typically it is used on a component that is using a better quality signal
    Satellite and Digital Cable TV Boxes
    SUPER-VHS VCRs
    DVD players, DVR/PVRs ,
    High 8 or better camcorders
    Better TVs

Find the rectangular connector and turn the cable to fit it in. The other pins will then push in easily.

THERE IS A DISTINCT WAY TO PUT IN THIS CONNECTION!

If you look head on at the cable connector end, there is a rectangular plastic piece that fits into the rectangular hole on the connection. By first checking how that lines up, you will be able to easily plug the cable in. (It could be either horizontally on top or bottom or vertically on one side.) **DO NOT FORCE THIS CABLE!!!** The pins are delicate and can bend or break off. This can be avoided by taking the moment to orient the cable before pushing it in.

A LESSON IN TELEVISION HISTORY THAT CAN HELP EXPLAIN HOW S-VIDEO WORKS...

You may remember (or have been told about) the early days of television when all TVs were black and white with shades of gray.

To create color television, the broadcasters sent red, green and blue signals (the primary colors of the light spectrum) to accompany the black and white signal. It is as though the color was laid on top of the black and white picture. The shades of gray in the black and white determined the color shades so that all color shades could realistically be shown on your home color TV.

A TV must receive the black and white and the color, and separate it out to shoot onto the display. If the TV can receive the information separately, there is less processing, the signal moves through the components with less interference and the result is a clearer picture with richer color.

One last thing about S-Video...

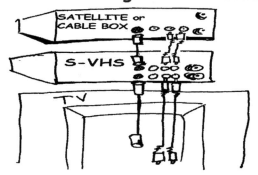

On S-VHS recorders, the signal can pass through just like the antenna pass through on regular VCRs. You may, however, have to go into to setup menu to turn on the pass-through option. When would you do this? To pass through the signal from a DVR, or a Digital Cable or Satellite box, to play when the S-VHS is powered off.

COMPONENT VIDEO
Also called: RGB connections

COMPONENT VIDEO uses 3 separate connections to make up the video signal. These analog cables are used for video from a digital source that has converted the signal to analog (see Chapter 2; "Digital to Analog"). Like S-Video, the component video is paired up with stereo (right and left) audio jacks, or digital audio. You must use component video connections (or another digital connection, described in the next section) with progressive scan DVD players when hooking up to a digital ready TV.

DVD component video OUTput

REASON FOR USE:

Like the S-Video cable, the component cables separate the luminance (brightness or "Y") from the color. Component cables take it one step further and separate each of the color signals. The green cable carries the luminance (or black and white version of the picture). The blue and red cables carry the other colors of the spectrum. It gives a superb picture in terms of clarity and realistic color—a less grainy picture with brighter whites and richer colors. It is especially noticeable with the use of digital signals like DVDs, digital and high definition TVs.

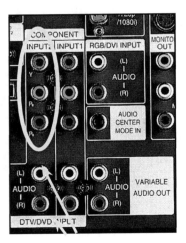

TV component video inputs—there are two. You'll use this component for DVD in the "DTV/DVD Input" (It's nice when it tells you what the inputs are used for!)

HOW TO SPOT THIS CONNECTION: (WHAT IT LOOKS LIKE)

It is easy to spot this connections. It look like RCA connections --they are raised with a circle in the center and they are grouped in 3, colored red, green and blue. But, when you stop to look at how they are labeled...The "Tower of Babble" is in effect. CURSES!

       You can find "Y", "Pb" and "Pr"
       You can find "Y", "Cb" and "Cr"
       You can find "Y" "B-Y" and "R-Y"
       You can find "Y" ,"U" ,"V"

But you're okay because you'll know what these connections are for!
"Y" is the green cable and it carries the brightness
Anything with "B" will be next to the blue connection.
Anything with "R" will be next to the red connection.

Just follow the colors!

A little warning...if you find 2 more connections near the red, green, and blue connections, which are labeled "H" and "V", go to the RGB-HV connections section.

DIGITAL & HDTV CONNECTIONS

If you have a digital or HDTV you will have different choices of connections to receive the ATSC (HDTV and EDTV) signal. Some of the cables run analog signals and others digital, if you have a choice, you will usually want to pick digital connections rather than analog. Read on.

Standardizing connections with HDTV
We are still in the early years of HDTV. As the manufacturers play with the best ways to send the signal from an HDTV tuner or other digital component, they work toward standardization that will provide both quality picture and sound and copyright protection.

Fear not, as the FCC is ensuring that current connections continue to be compatible with connections as things progress.

Section 3: Analog Video Connections for HDTV

What? Analog connections for a digital TV?
We see in analog so the digital signal will have to be converted at some point so that we can see the picture. (See HDTV Chapter 2 converting digital to analog signals.) Sending digital signals on a digital connection is your first choice for high quality, but some components are lagging behind and only offer analog connections. For those devices, you will probably find the following analog connections.

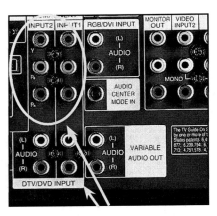

TV component video inputs--there are two. Note that it tells you it is for "DTV/DVD Input" (It's nice when it tells you what the inputs are used for!)

COMPONENT VIDEO
(SEE PREVIOUS SECTION FOR COMPLETE INFORMATION.)

Some HDTVs hook up to their set-top decoder/tuners through simple component video. On the back of a DTV or HDTV you will look for the component jacks to have a specific label of" DTV "or "HDTV".

On these TVs you will often also have an input for a DVD player—which will not be high definition, but will usually have a component video input/output.

Be sure to pay attention to hook up a DVD or other NTSC analog signal device to the component video in labeled for its use. And be sure to hook up any HDTV or DTV signal to the component video labeled for that.

CHECK YOUR COMPONENT VIDEO INPUTS CAREFULLY:

There may be more than one component video input on a TV. For the TV to properly use the progressive scan signal, you must connect the component video connection that is labeled for progressive scan. There may also be an input that is labeled for HDTV. When making note of the connections on your TV, be sure to note what each input is labeled so that you can connect it to the correct device. (See HDTV chapter 2, "Progressive Scan".)

RGB-HV

Also called "RGB with horizontal sync."

The **RGB-HV** connection can be found on some of the first High Definition set top tuner boxes. It is like a standard component (RGB) cable with the addition of "H" and "V" cables which are for horizontal and vertical synchronization (helps it to reproduce the original signal so they are at the same speed). Many times the high definition set top box has an RGB connection. (See RGB/ VGA below.)–like a computer monitor/ VGA type, and then TV has the RGB-HV 5 terminal input. Refer to Cables Chapter 4 for the right cable to use.

REASON FOR USE:

These cables are used with high definition and digital formats. Often the five cables have professional connectors called "**BNC**" (that locks onto the connection) instead of the typical RCA phono plug connectors. The connections include separation of color and luminance (as described in component cables) with the addition of a horizontal sync and a vertical sync. This keeps the picture clear and without interference (called "artifacts").

This is a "BNC" connector and is used in place of a phono plug "RCA" connector. It is common to find RGBHV using BNC plugs. You can buy BNC cables or get "female phono pin to BNC" adapters at your local accessory store that converts RCA cables to BNC.

HOW TO SPOT THIS CONNECTION: (WHAT IT LOOKS LIKE)

Like a component video DTV connection, this connection may be clearly labeled HDTV or DTV. The red, green and blue video terminals will be grouped with an extra two RCA connectors—so, it will commonly have green, red, blue and yellow and white. The yellow here is *not* the same as a composite yellow video cable. It may have the red, green and blue and two other connections of any color, you will be able to tell by the labels "H" and "V". If the grouping were green, red, blue, RED and white, it could be a simple component video with an analog audio jack. Note labels to be sure. It could be labeled Y,Pr,Pb,GR,B,HV. Pay attention to lines around groupings and labels.

EQUIPMENT ON WHICH YOU MIGHT FIND THIS CONNECTION:

Other than professional use, this connection is used to connect a
High Definition Tuner/set top box to a
High Definition Rear Projection TV

Digital connections for HDTV

HDMI is a newcomer to connections but has promise of becoming the standard for HDTV and digital signal.

HDMI
("HIGH DEFINITION MULTIMEDIA INTERFACE")

The name of this connection is the first clue that this connection carries digital video AND audio connection. HDMI is the behemoth of high definition digital connections. It can carry all of the uncompressed high definition video signal AND 8 channels of digital audio (*and* there's room to spare for future information).

REASON FOR USE:

This connection is used to transmit digital video and audio signals. Movie makers particularly like it because it will carry copy protection. That is, it has HDCP or High Definition Copy Protection capabilities. There is talk that it **may** become the DTV standard connection of the future. **An HDMI connection can be hooked up to a DVI-HDCP** if that is what is available on your other component. (DVI will need an additional audio cable as it carries only video signal.) You will need a DVI to HDMI cable. (See Cables Chapter.)

HOW TO SPOT THIS CONNECTION:
(WHAT IT LOOKS LIKE)

This connection has a raised center to fit into the cable similar to that of a USB connection on a computer. It will be labeled HDMI and is angled in at the bottom corners rather than square like a USB. It is considerably smaller than a DVI connection.

EQUIPMENT ON WHICH YOU MIGHT FIND THIS CONNECTION:

HDMI OUTput on a DVD player. Note that it is much smaller than the DVI connection.

High definition tuners/set top box
High definition TVs
DVD players (standard definition DVD too)
...and more every day!

You will *not* find HDMI on a purely analog source like a stand alone VCR.

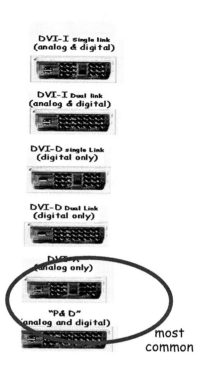

DVI-I single link
(analog & digital)

DVI-I Dual link
(analog & digital)

DVI-D single Link
(digital only)

DVI-D Dual Link
(digital only)

DVI-A
(analog only)

"P&D"
(analog and digital)

most
common

DVI:
Also called: Digital Video Interface, **DVI-HDCP,**
DVI-A DVI-I, DVI-D

A relative newcomer on the market, this connection has the capability to send HDTV information. It can send either analog or digital signals. It is a pin connection and like a VGA (like computer monitor), may have screws on either side to keep the connection secure, and prevent the pins from bending.

Unlike HDMI, DVI is a *video only connection* and will be grouped with audio connections. While most new equipment is digital, you want to be sure that connections on both pieces of equipment match digital to digital or analog to analog. (See illustration). A DVI-A cable can only carry analog signals. A DVI-D cable can only carry digital signals. The DVI-I cable will carry either analog or digital but not at the same time. "DVI-HDCP" stands for DIGITAL VIDEO INTERFACE-HIGH DEFINITION COPY PROTECTION" and is a digital connection, **with the proper cable, this connection can be hooked up to an HDMI on the other end. But you must also hook up audio when connecting a video-only DVI to HDMI.**

REASON FOR USE:
It is used on High Definition and Digital Televisions. It transports digital signals with impressive power efficiency and low noise, and as a result is an excellent connection for picture quality with HDTV. Remember though, unlike HDMI, DVI is video only.

HOW TO SPOT THIS CONNECTION:
(WHAT IT LOOKS LIKE)

This is a pin connection (think s-vhs has pins) so look for the holes. It is shaped similar to a VGA connection. It will be labeled DVI. To determine if your connection is analog or digital see the illustration to the left.

While most DVI connections on new HDTV products will be digital...Be sure that you only connect analog to analog or digital to digital. The connections on both the output of the device and the input of the TV or second device **must** match.

HDMI OUTPUT ON A DVD PLAYER. Can you tell what kind of DVI it is? If you count the rows you will see 8 across and 3 down or a DVI-D digital as shown on the illustration to the left.

iEEE1394 (AUDIO AND VIDEO)
ALSO CALLED: FIREWIRE, iLINK®*, DTVLINK™

This is another connection that came about from the computer world. It is a purely digital connection that is **BI-DIRECTIONAL,** that is, it can be both an input and an output *through a single connection.* It talks both ways.

REASON FOR USE:

A firewire can transmit both digital video and digital audio with just one connection and can send information in and out through the same terminal and cable. While some manufacturers adopted this connection, HDMI is said to be capable of carrying more information. Some manufacturers have chosen this connection to ensure that all of their components have an easy integration. Most digital camcorders can be connected through iEEE1394. This allows you to watch your movies on your HDTV. It is especially useful when this connection is on the front of a DVD recorder, as it allows you to make quick DVD copies of your home movies for a high quality archive.

HOW TO SPOT THIS CONNECTION:
(WHAT IT LOOKS LIKE)

The iEEE1394 cable can be as wide as a USB but the four pin connections are very small indeed. It will be labeled iEEE1394 or the other names listed above. Occasionally it will bear the symbol seen in the illustration.

EQUIPMENT ON WHICH YOU MIGHT FIND THIS CONNECTION:

Same brand TVs and components
Digital VCRs
DVD recorders
Computers
Digital camcorders
Digital cameras

Note: if you find this connection on an A/V receiver, it is probably intended as a digital audio connection. (See following digital audio section.) Be sure to check your manual and make note of any nearby labels.

Using your TV as a monitor (ANALOG CONNECTION)

RGB/VGA

ALSO CALLED: JUST RGB OR VGA, XGA OR SVGA, HD15 D-SUB

This connection comes from the computer world. It is the connection used from your monitor to your computer. When found on digital and high definition televisions, it is often used to connect your computer to your TV so it can be used instead of a monitor.

REASON FOR USE:

While this connection can hook up to an RGB-HV connection, it is typically used to hook up your computer monitor. This is done to get a larger screen or to use a display in a room with only a TV. Front projectors can show a presentation on a large screen for a group.

CAUTION: Take care if using a Plasma to display a computer desktop or other static image (See chapter 2, "Burn In".)

HOW TO SPOT THIS CONNECTION: (WHAT IT LOOKS LIKE)

A pin connection labeled "RGB" or "VGA" or "SVGA" or "XGA" or any combination.

EQUIPMENT ON WHICH YOU MIGHT FIND THIS CONNECTION:

Computers
LCD flat panel monitors and TVs
Front Projection Televisions
HD ready TVs
Occasionally on HD set top boxes
Occasionally on Direct View Digital TVs

AUDIO CONNECTIONS

SECTION 4: Audio Connections

As with video connections, there are different jacks for connecting the sound (audio) to your TV, components or home theater A/V receiver. The connections might be analog or digital and carry different types of sound, mono, stereo, Dolby Pro Logic® Surround, Dolby Digital® Surround, dts, DVD-Audio or SACD.

RCA

ALSO CALLED: LINE AUDIO

As covered in the section on RCA video connections, these are the red (right) and white (left) audio information. These hookups will give you stereo through right and left channels (speakers). It can also carry signals for Dolby Pro Logic® Surround or dts: Neo 6™ surround sound but cannot send the digital signal needed for Dolby Digital® or dts surround sound (See HDTV chapter 2, HDTV Audio Format.")

REASON FOR USE:

This connection separates stereo, right and left channels. They can be matrixed (encoded) for surround sound. It is used to send analog audio signals.

HOW TO SPOT THIS CONNECTION: (WHAT IT LOOKS LIKE)

You can recognize these inputs as Audio R and L usually with red for right and white for left. They can be alone, for an audio player like CD or tape player, or combined with video of any kind.

More will be explained in the cables section as the quality of RCA cables can make a great difference.

EQUIPMENT ON WHICH YOU MIGHT FIND THIS CONNECTION:

Found on just about every piece of equipment that uses audio from TVs to stereos to DVDs (and when it's not found, it is usually connected to a head-phone connection on one end and RCA on another).

Digital Audio Connections

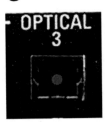

TosLink- DIGITAL OPTICAL AUDIO
AKA: OPTICAL AUDIO CABLE; FIBER-OPTIC AUDIO

This connection sends and receives digital audio signals as light pulses that travel over a **FIBER-OPTIC** TosLink cable. "**TOSLINK**" gets its name from Toshiba who developed this cable/connection.

REASON FOR USE:

As with coaxial digital cables, this is a digital audio connection. Often it is sending Dolby Digital® or dts surround sound information to your home theater A/V receiver. Your receiver must have a built in decoder for Dolby Digital® or dts. A/V receivers will usually be labeled with the logos of the formats which it can decode.

HOW TO SPOT THIS CONNECTION: (WHAT IT LOOKS LIKE)

The connection for TosLink is usually covered with a plastic plug that can be easily removed by grabbing its little protrusion. Once uncovered, you can spot the red laser light that is used to transmit the signal. Keep it covered if you are not using it to keep the connection free from dust, etc. You'll want to match the notches and the flat side of the cable for easiest connection. If you connect a fiber optic cable, you can see the red laser light at the other end of the cable (it's best not to stare at the light).

EQUIPMENT ON WHICH YOU MIGHT FIND THIS CONNECTION:

    Home Theater Receivers
    DVD players and DVD Recorders,
    Satellite or Digital Cable Box
    DVRs
    HDTVs and HDTV components

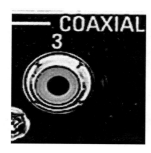

COAXIAL—
DIGITAL AUDIO

This is a connection that uses a coaxial cable similar to the yellow video RCA cable. More will be covered in the cables chapter.

REASON FOR USE:

This is a digital audio connection. It can send Dolby Digital® or dts surround sound information to your home theater A/V receiver. Your receiver must have a built in decoder for Dolby Digital®or dts in order to separate and play these digital surround formats. When a device sends a digital signal to the receiver, the receiver must convert the digital signal to analog. A/V receivers will usually be labeled on front with the logos of the formats which it can decode.

HOW TO SPOT THIS CONNECTION:
(WHAT IT LOOKS LIKE)

This connection uses a phono plug much like the RCA jacks. The ring will typically be colored **orange** or **black** and may be labeled "**PCM**". "**BITSTREAM**", "Coaxial", or "Digital Audio".

EQUIPMENT ON WHICH YOU MIGHT FIND THIS CONNECTION:

Home Theater Receivers
DVD players and DVD Recorders,
Satellite or Digital Cable TV Box,
DVRs
HDTVs and HDTV components

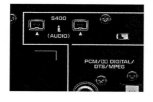

IEEE1394
(FOR DIGITAL AUDIO)

This is an up and coming connection to carry digital audio. It is used in circumstances where the DVD decodes and separates the signal and then passes the digital audio on to an A/V receiver. This is used in place of 6 or 8 channel line audio (and will probably have more uses as time goes on). Read the explanation of 6 or 8 channel line audio for more information.

At the time of this book's publication, iEEE1394 digital audio connections could only be found on high end a/v receivers and DVD players and DVD recorders.

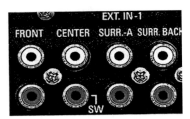

This is an example of an 8 channel input. Like RCA stereo audio connections, you will use only one jack for each channel. The white and red jack labeled "front" will be for left and right front channels (respectively).

You will use one white for the left front speaker and one red for the right front speaker. You will want to match ouputs from your device with inputs on your a/v home theater receiver.

Note that one white input is for the center channel and the red is marked "sw" for subwoofer.

6 (OR 8) CHANNEL LINE AUDIO

When this connection is used, it sends analog audio to the receiver/amplifier. A separate connection is used for each speaker. For 6 channels the connections are for front right, front left, surround right, surround left, center, LFE (subwoofer) For 8 channel, add surround back right and surround back left.

Components, particularly DVD players, which read digital audio from CDs or DVDs, can either convert the signal to analog or send the signal out through a digital connection where the receiver/amplifier converts the signal to analog. (See HDTV chapter 2 Converting analog to digital and digital to analog or Digital and analog information and section 6 HDTV Audio Format for surround sound explanation.)

Before choosing this connection, find out if the decoder is in the DVD player or does the receiver/amplifier. Second, does the home theater receiver have a 6 (or 8) channel audio input?

REASON FOR USE:
When DVD players first came out, receivers could send out signal to 5.1 surround speakers but did not have decoders built in to read the Dolby Digital®or dts information. The DVD would have to convert the signals then send it out through the separate analog cables. The receiver only had to amplify the sound and pass it on to the speakers. Today, Dolby Digital® and dts is commonly decoded in the A/V receiver and 6 channel line inputs are not required.

New surround formats are again requiring line inputs. DVD players can play DVD Audio, SACD, and HDCD, where not all a/v receivers have decoders. Again, the 6 or 8 channel line audios are used when the receiver cannot decode the signal.

HOW TO SPOT THIS CONNECTION: (WHAT IT LOOKS LIKE)
You will find 6 or 8 red and white jacks together. It will be labeled "6 (or 8) channel in", or "EXT. In" or line in. Look for the speaker labels "front, center, sw" etc., otherwise it could be just a lot of audio connections near each other. Be sure to read the name.

EQUIPMENT ON WHICH YOU MIGHT FIND THIS CONNECTION:
Home Theater Receivers
DVD players and DVD Recorders,

SECTION 5: Other Connections You Might Find

Today's TVs are used for more than TV broadcasts—for movies and slide shows and media players—more connections are added for future use. Some components use special connections to synchronize with other equipment or to receive information from computers through phone lines.

TELEPHONE: Used on Satellite and Cable TV boxes, as well as some DVRs. The phone line for Satellite and Cable TV make it possible to order pay per view movies with your remote. (The phone calls a computer that unlocks your account to let you see the movie.) On DVRs, the phone line is used by the component's modem to receive programming information. This allows you to go to the guide and pick a program in the future or on another channel and with a button, chose to record it or get a season pass.

ETHERNET-(RJ-45): Allows for connecting with your home computer network or to a device that creates a wireless network. This connection is showing up on newer televisions and home media components.

MINI-PLUG SYNC: It synchronizes products from the same brand -(Sony to Sony, JVC to JVC), especially used in recording devices like VCRs.

RS-232: This is like the computer connection. It is used for one device to control another—a DVR can be hooked into a Satellite or Cable TV box so that it can change the channel that you want to record. It may have additional uses consult your owner's manual.

USB: Coming from the computer world, this allows you to hook up devices typically used with computers to TVs, DVDs, DVD-Rs, DVRs and web TVs . It can be hooked into a wireless device, home media center or computer. It can also be used to hook up portable USB information devices which carry media. The use of this connection is still being developed.

MEDIA CARD SLOTS AND CD DRIVES: This is a new feature on some digital TVs, DVD Recorders and more. It allows you to plug in your digital camera's memory card so that you can view a slide show of photos on your TV with ease.

Section 6: Real World Examples...Practice!

The following are real world examples of connection panels ("jack packs") that you might find on various components. Going through the following photos will give you an idea of various configurations you might encounter. It will give you practice and comfort when you are faced with a large number of jacks.

No need to panic. Just have a pen and paper and go section by section. Note all the connections you find in an area that might be outlined and labeled "inputs" or "outputs".

The more you look at your equipment and practice finding the inputs and outputs the easier it will be. It can even become a game (well, one could hope to have fun!)

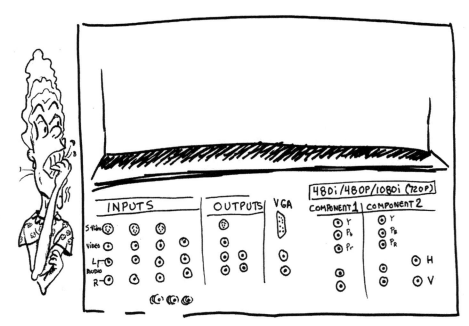

Inputs on traditional Direct View picture tube TVs are found on the back of the TV. As you'll see some flat panel TVs have the main inputs and outputs hidden on the side of the TV. Today's TVs have gotten tricky by placing some connections on the side or top walls of the "jack panels" where other inputs are located.

Look around. Pay attention to labels, to lines, to numbers. Labels and numbers will help you to know which input your TV is displaying (it will come up briefly on the screen) and sometimes what you can hook up to that input (when labeled HDTV or DVD etc.). The lines surrounding a group of jacks make up one input. Audio and video connections grouped within lined areas are usually one input or used for one component to be connected.

Don't be alarmed if you get confused when looking at the following pictures of inputs and outputs. When you look at your equipment, if something doesn't seem right to you, it's time to pull out the manual. For example, we know that HDMI carries both video AND audio signal. *So, why would it be grouped with an audio input?* Consulting the manual shows us that you can hook up a device which has a DVI connection to a TV that has only an HDMI input. This is done by using a cable with DVI on one end and HDMI on the other (see Digital Video cables in "Cables" Chapter). DVI carries only video; therefore, the audio inputs that are grouped with the HDMI input are to be used when connecting a DVI to HDMI cable for the video.

DIRECT VIEW TVs

Pay attention to lines, labels and numbers. Here it is labeled "video in" and "1", "3" and "4" (video input 2 is on the front of the TV).

Photo courtesy of Sony Electronics

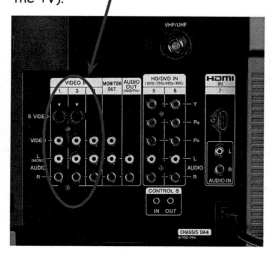

FLAT PANEL TVs

Flat screens sometimes have the main connections on the side of the TV so that it can lay flat against the wall as in the illustration on this page.

Other flat screens like the Toshiba below, have the main connections recessed on the back.

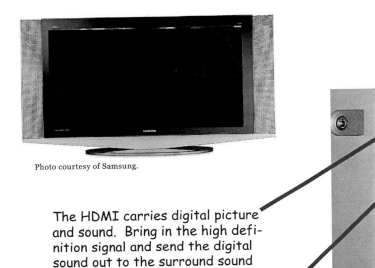

Photo courtesy of Samsung.

On both of these flat screens there are side connections to use for video games, camcorders etc.

The HDMI carries digital picture and sound. Bring in the high definition signal and send the digital sound out to the surround sound receiver.

The DVI input carries only video. Note the audio input to use with the DVI.

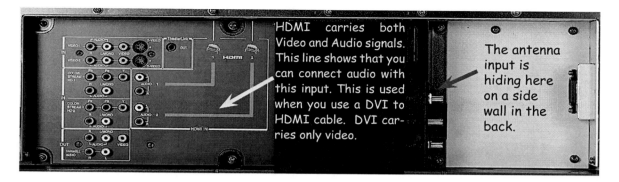

HDMI carries both Video and Audio signals. This line shows that you can connect audio with this input. This is used when you use a DVI to HDMI cable. DVI carries only video.

The antenna input is hiding here on a side wall in the back.

Photo courtesy of Sony Electronics

Front connections behind "push to open" panel is good for video games, camcorders or digital cameras.

Check out how this Sony television has turned the jacks so they point downward. Still, they are labeled. The VHF/UHF antenna connection's label is embossed above the terminal.

You can connect your center channel speaker connection to this TV. The TV speakers then act as the center speaker for your surround system. (It's better to have front speakers with matched quality. So while it is convenient, you probably wouldn't choose this connection—see Surround Sound in HDTV chapter.)

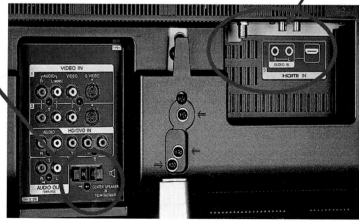

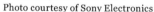

VCRs

Often a VCR will have a line of the inputs and a line of outputs. You can choose RF cable pass-through or if you have an S-VHS you can pick S-Video pass-through. Don't PANIC. If you didn't understand all that, check out Chapter 1, Section 5 "pass-through signals" and the Hookup Preparation Chapter 5, "Tips and Rules". Also, you'll get more information to make your decision after going through the cables chapter. The answers are here.

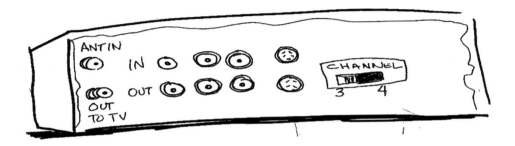

DISH Satellite AND DVR COMBO

The only input on this unit is from the satellite dish via RG6 coaxial cable. Some units can split the signal to 2 tuners internally others need two RF coaxial cable inputs.

Pay close attention to labels... this satellite receiver can accept local channels from antenna or cable.

This unit connects to a TV in a second room. (See explanation in Chapter 1 Dual tuner satellites.)

There are 2 RCA outputs. One to go to your TV, the other to VHS or DVD-recorder. or you can use the RF connection to your TV or you can hook up out via s-video for better picture quality.

DVDs

Some DVDs group the video outputs together and the audio outputs together. Choose one video output and to be sure that you hear all DVDs, not just the Dolby Digital® and dts discs, hook up both a digital audio connection **and** the RCA line audio.

These two DVD players illustrate how differently jack panels can be designed. Be sure to look around and read labels. The top DVD player is manufactured by Denon and the bottom is a Yamaha model.

HOME THEATER "A/V" RECEIVER

Practice finding connections like putting together a puzzle. You won't find waldo but maybe...
you can find a component video connection for your DVD

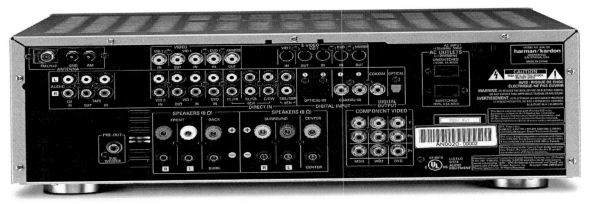

Photo courtesy of Harmon Kardon.

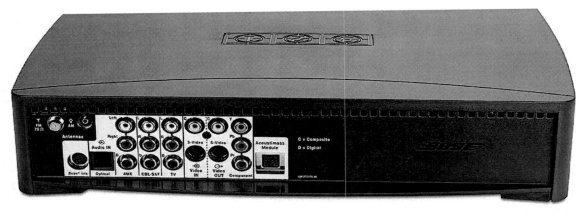

This is a Bose home theater system. As you can read the jacks labeled "D" is for digital audio, coaxial cables. The audio inputs are separate from the video. There is a choice of RCA composite video or S-video in; and a choice of RCA composite video or S-video or Component video out...we would have to read the manual to understand how there could be a component video output without a component video input.

Also note the "Bose link" and "Acoustimass" special connections for the speakers.

No, I'm not kidding. This Denon receiver is actually well organized.

If you slow down, you can find the inputs and ouputs on a receiver like this (one like I used as a model for the cover illustration). First, let's see how they organized the receiver. They have put all of the audio inputs in one section and video in a section next to it. See the vertical rows of red and white jacks? Each are labeled with a different device name. They are grouped in a box that is labeled "in". Can you find the audio in for the DVD? Can you find an audio input for VCR-1. Now look to the right of the audio jacks. There is a column of yellow RCA video inputs and S-video inputs, again labeled with device names. You can hook up a device other than what is named but you'll want to make note of the label (i.e. hooking up a DVD recorder to the VCR-1 jack) because you will be switching to that component by what the label says.

Look around some more. Do you see the component video inputs on the top right? You can hook up 3 different devices to the component video inputs. These connections are for video only. The connection labeled "monitor" and "out" will connect out to the TV's input. Often these are "assignable" connections and you may need to tell the receiver which devices are connected to them. You'll usually find that in the setup menu of your a/v receiver.

If you want to receive the sound from the device you connected with component video you will have to choose an audio connection as well. Most devices using component video will have digital sound for Dolby Digital® or Dts™ surround sound. As you explore, to the far left you find some inputs for "opt" which are numbered. "Opt" stands for "optical" (TosLink or optical digital sound cable). There are also "coax" connections for digital coaxial sound cables (which you might choose instead of the optical in connection). The tip here is that at the bottom of that box of inputs is a label "in" and "digital". Again you may need to tell the receiver which device is connected by going into the a/v receiver's setup menu. You will also find a group of 8 red and white audio cables with "FR, FL, SW, SR, Sl, SBR, SBL." These are for the 6 or 8 channel input for DVD Audio and SACD. It is labeled "EXT In".

As you familiarize yourself more, check the speaker connections. Each speaker will have a positive and negative connection. (Sometimes the subwoofer has a different cable connection.) This high end receiver has two sets of surround speakers that can be used for speakers in another room.

Untangling the Web of Cables

WHAT YOU WILL LEARN IN CHAPTER 4...

-How to choose the connection and cable that is best for your TV.

-What makes a high quality cable.

-How to identify a cable.

-How to measure for the right length cable.

-Matching quality of cables to your equipment.

Words to know in this chapter:

802.11
900 MHZ
BITSTREAM
BNC CONNECTORS
CHROMA
COAX
COAXIAL AUDIO
COMPONENT VIDEO
DIGITAL AUDIO
DIGITAL SURROUND SOUND
DOLBY DIGITAL
DTS™
DVD AUDIO
DVI-DIGITAL VISUAL INTERFACE
FIBER OPTIC CABLES
FIREWIRE
HDMI-HIGH   DEFINITION   MULTIMEDIA   INTER-
FACE
IEEE1394
INTERCONNECTS
LINE AUDIO
LUMINANCE
OPTICAL AUDIO CABLE
PCM
RCA COMPOSITE CABLES
RF CABLE
RG-6 CABLE
RGB
SPLIT PIN RCA CONNECTOR
SVGA, XVGA
S-VIDEO
TOSLINK
VGA
WI-FI
Y/C CABLE

Section 1: Considering Cables: "Interconnects"

All cables are not created equal. Different cables, connectors, how the cable is constructed, all contribute to how well a signal is carried from one component to the next. How well a signal arrives at its destination device determines the quality of picture and sound.

WHY SHOULD I CARE ABOUT CABLES?

Whether your picture is coming from an antenna, Cable TV, DVD, VCR, DVR, Satellite, or any place else, it needs to leave its source and arrive at your TV. Cables connect the output of one device to the input of the next device or TV. No matter how well the source creates a great picture, your top-of-the-line DVD player for example, that picture has to arrive at your TV without dropping signal or picking up interference along the way.

Quality cable connectors are essential to good signal transfer

No matter how good the picture is at the source, it must go through a cable and arrive at your TV without interference or dropping signal.

What happens when cables are unable to carry all the signal that the source is providing? Picture and sound quality suffer. (We'll focus on video for now.) At its worst, there can be ghost images, snowy interference, color bands, blurry or low contrast, dark pictures, or digital boxes ("artifacts") that appear on screen.

Sometimes cables are included in the box with your equipment purchase. Mostly, these cables are the simplest cables that can do the job of running the picture and sound. You can tell just by looking at them that their flimsy, thin construction is just a step up from the electrical wire that runs the power from the wall.

If you are using sub-standard cable, it can pick up interference from electrical wires, or any other frequency in the air, like a radio station or a broadcast that reaches your home. What appears is degraded picture quality.

What makes a good quality cable?

Companies that make quality cables have piles of technical literature containing lists of specifications on cables. "Dielectric" "foam core" "oxygen-free"...all sound more techie than most of us care about. What's the bottom line?

The construction of the cable makes a difference in transferring the sound and picture and makes a difference at how well it keeps out interference.

The elements that make a difference in the performance of a cable are:

- What metal the wire/cable makes up the cable. (Usually copper and "Oxygen-free" copper is better).

- How those wires are twisted and the number of wires that make up the cable. (Some are even twisted to run the signal in a particular direction and have arrows to point toward their destination).

- How well the cable is shielded from outside interference.

- What kind of metal makes up the end connectors and

- How well they connect to the terminals A loose connection loses information/ signal before it reaches its destination.

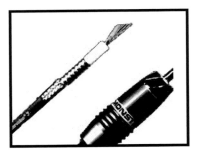

This composite video cable is surrounded by a plastic coating, a layer of metal shielding and then braided metal.

These are examples of how cables are shielded against interference.

In this photo of an S-Video cable you can see the separate cables that carry the chroma and the luminance. Each is separately shielded.

Quality cable photos courtesy of Monster Cable Products, Inc.

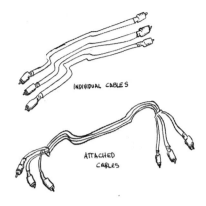

INDIVIDUAL CABLES

ATTACHED CABLES

SPAGHETTI CABLES

Many people make the mistake of opening their new component, taking out the included cables and hooking it up. The result is picture and/or sound is less than what they saw in the store. Often the included cables are little better than a lamp cord that carries electricity and are often referred to as "spaghetti cable" for their thin, flimsy construction.

Getting the information *to* the next device or TV is half the battle. A cable that does not connect securely will have a signal that cuts out. You may have noticed cables that have "gold connectors". Gold can conduct (send) a signal better than lesser metals. Again, cables are about getting signal (information) from one device to the next. You want all of the information to arrive. Gold connectors that are designed to create a snug fit by twisting on, or split pins that make better contact are worth the extra expense.

The construction of the cable can also encourage the signal to flow directly and completely to its destination. Be sure you aren't using the flimsy spaghetti-like cables that come in the box with your component. Quality of picture and sound may be lost.

EXAMPLES OF CABLE CONNECTORS

included cables

upgraded cables

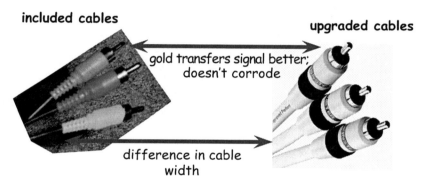

gold transfers signal better; doesn't corrode

difference in cable width

Upgrading cables to better cables will give big results. Note the difference in width (shielding of these included cables than the upgraded cables). The included cables use inferior metals which will not send the signal as efficiently and can corrode relatively quickly ruining not only picture or sound quality, but the jack on your device!

These quality cables use gold and a turbine, twist-on end to connect securely to the device's input or output. Split pins insure contact with the jack, all creating superior signal transfer. Be careful to twist these cables off (not pull). These connections are so snug they'll pull the jack right out of the device..

Section 2: Picking the right video cable for your connection

You have inspected your equipment to discover which connections are available on each of your components. Below are illustrations which pair the connections with their cable partners. In the following pages each cable will be described along with recommendations for their use.

STANDARD ANALOG TV CONNECTIONS

TYPE	IF YOU HAVE THIS CONNECTION.	USE THIS CABLE.	RECOMMENDATION:
RF (F-PIN) (VIDEO AND AUDIO)			Use to bring in picture from outside. Use between devices only if you have *no other option*. (Other than running digital signals for Satellite or cable: **Maximum 330 lines out of possible 480 lines of resolution.**)
RCA (COMPOSITE) (USUALLY COMBINED WITH LINE AUDIO)			Stereo sound and better picture resolution . Full 480 lines of resolution. **Choose if nothing better.**
S-VIDEO			Video is separated into color and brightness (chroma and luminance). **Gives clearer picture with better color.**
COMPONENT VIDEO			Best connection analog can offer. Colors are further separated making them even richer, brighter. **BEST CHOICE when available.**

AND THE DIGITAL/HIGH DEFINITION GANG...

Type	If you have this connection.	Use this cable.	Recommendation:
COMPONENT VIDEO			For High Definition, component video cable is the basic cable to use. As an analog connection, it can lose picture quality.
RGB-HV			Some High Definition set top boxes have an RGB connector on one end and connects to the TV with 5 cables May have 5 connections on both ends or RGB on one and 5 connections on other. **Choose it if you need it for your connections**.
IEEE1394 (ILINK, DTVLINK™, FIREWIRE)			This cable can carry PICTURE AND SOUND but cannot carry as much information as HDMI. D-VHS uses this connection, as does some HD cable boxes. Choose it if you can't choose HDMI.
DVI	DVI-I Dual link		DVI is either an analog OR digital video connection resulting in excellent picture quality. Be sure to match your components (both analog or both digital). Does not carry audio. **Good choice but some say they like HDMI better.**
HDMI (VIDEO AND AUDIO)			Digital AUDIO AND VIDEO. Can send a lot of information. The more information, the less loss of pictures and sound quality. **BEST CHOICE when available.**

Presenting...The Cables!

A coaxial cable has a single copper core surrounded by insulation. The core wire extends out (f-pin). Above it is threaded onto its connection, below is a push on type.

The cable that connects from the wall plate is a coaxial cable. Be sure it is an "RG-6" type of cable for digital Cable TV or Satellite. It is marked along the length of the cable.

RF (RADIO FREQUENCY)
COMMON NAMES:
COAXIAL CABLE, F-PIN, "COAX", ANTENNA CABLE

USES:
Found on all equipment that can display or record a broadcast or outside signal.

Connecting from antenna, Cable TV or Satellite dish, and from wall to Cable TV box, Satellite receiver or straight to TV or recorder (VCR, DVD recorder or DVR/PVR).

Can be used between Cable TV box/Satellite receiver and VCR, DVR and/or TV (*not preferred*)..

May be the only input on inexpensive or older televisions.

LIMITATIONS:
Picture is least favorable. While an analog coaxial cable's maximum resolution is 330 lines, digital Cable TV and Satellite broadcast over 425 lines. Cannot carry stereo and therefore will not carry any type of surround sound.

Note: There is a difference between the analog coax cable that is used between devices and that RG-6 cable that carries digital signal into the set top box. The RG-6 carries digital information and does not lose picture quality and can carry stereo sound.

BENEFITS:
Easy hookup. Single line for sound and picture. Found on almost every TV.

RECOMMENDATIONS:
Use when bringing signal from wall and for PIP. (See Chapter 1, "Dual Tuners and P.I.P.") Choose another input if available.

VARIATIONS:
Screw on pin cable or push on for older TVs. The push-on is not as secure, which can lead to picture loss or can become easily disconnected.

**Yellow-video,
Red-right audio and
White-left audio**

(Occasionally blue instead of white).

Plastic ends can be fully yellow (or red or white) or they may just have a band of color to indicate which is which.

The bands on these Monster Cables indicate if the cable is video, or audio left or right Note that this left cable is marked with a blue band instead of white.

RCA/COMPOSITE
COMMON NAMES:
COMPOSITE, AUDIO/VIDEO or "A/V" CABLES

USES:
Connecting equipment with video and stereo sound. Use out of Satellite receiver , Cable TV box, VCRs, video games, web TV, DVR/PVRs and more. Can be used with DVDs and camcorders. Always choose your hookup by what's available *and* use the best available which fits into your budget.

LIMITATIONS:
This cable is better than an RF cable, but it is still a composite video cable. The luminance (brightness) and the chroma (color) are combined and there is a loss of picture quality compared to S-video or component video which separate out the signal. (See following sections). This cable has a maximum 450 lines or resolution which is most, but not all, of an NTSC signal.

BENEFITS:
Because RCA cables separate the audio and video signals, it has more resolution than RF/f-pin coaxial cables. This will give you the full resolution of the incoming picture. It will look sharper. Also, the audio cables carry stereo sound and basic Surround Sound. (See HDTV chapter 2, "HDTV audio formats.")

RECOMMENDATIONS/VARIATIONS:
The quality of these cables can vary greatly. The spaghetti-thin cables that come with the product have no true shielding and easily picking up interference. The picture is less defined, has less contrast. The sound cables lose frequencies and sound isn't true and rich.

The better the source (DVDs, digital Cable TV/Satellite receivers), the better the cable you should look for. If you choose RCA cables, choose higher grade cables that offer snug connectors that need to be twisted on and off to insure full picture and sound transfer from cable to connection.

RCA cables are better than an "RF" because they separate sound and picture, but not as good as S-video or component that separate the color elements.

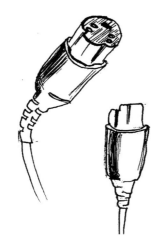

S-VIDEO
COMMON NAMES:
Y/C CABLE, S-VHS CABLE (TERM IS INCORRECTLY USED BUT USED NONETHELESS)

USES:
Connecting video equipment with a higher quality output. Satellite Receivers, some digital Cable TV, high 8 camcorders, DVD players, Super VHS recorders, and DVRs.

LIMITATIONS:
Only component video gives you a cleaner analog picture. Not available on all TVs, may need to upgrade to a higher quality TV for this input. You need to be careful when inserting and removing the cable to be sure not to bend the delicate pins. It can show full NTSC resolution.

BENEFITS:
Because it separates the brightness and color (which must be done to display a color picture on your TV), there is less processing when it reaches your TV.

You get a brighter, sharper picture with richer color than with an RCA cable.

RECOMMENDATIONS:
Quality of S-video cable can vary. A high end S-Video cable is often so good that it is hard to distinguish picture quality when compared to a low end component cable.

Again, do not use the spaghetti-thin cable that may have come with the product.

Remember, S-Video only carries the video signal. Choose either RCA line audio cables or a digital audio cable for digital surround sound from a DVD or Satellite or Cable TV box.

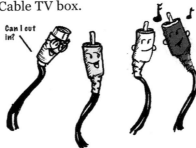

Component video cables or digital video cables must be used to get the "progressive scan" signal from a DVD. (You must also have a TV capable of showing progressive scan
(See HDTV chapter 2 How TVs work-- "progressive scan".)

COMPONENT VIDEO CABLES
OCCASIONALLY CALLED:
RGB VIDEO CABLES

USES:
Connecting from a digital source that has converted the picture to an analog signal, to a TV. Mainly found on DVDs, and high definition components.

These cables send ANALOG signals. The digital signal must be converted by a Cable TV or Satellite box or a DVD player before it is sent through these cables to the TV.

LIMITATIONS:
For most people who have NTSC (that is, *not high definition*) TVs, these cables are the best you can get.

For high definition and digital TVs: Although more home theater amplifiers are coming with component inputs and outputs, if you are using these cables with a high definition signal, be sure your amplifier can transfer the component signal (to be sure, check the manual). (See Hookup Chapter 5, "Upconversion a/v Receiver".)

BENEFITS:
3 cables separate brightness (luminance) and send the color (chroma) signals down separate cables which results in a beautiful, sharp picture with excellent contrast and vibrant color.

RECOMMENDATIONS:
If this connection is available on your analog TV and other equipment, **take advantage of it!**

As with RCA and S-video cables, quality cables will give you quality picture. Don't substitute cheap component cables for a good S-video. It will be hard to tell the difference. If you are upgrading, get a good cable.

High Definition Video Cables

If one component has a DVI connection, you can still take advantage of hdmi by using a "DVI to hdmi cable" which has the different connections at each end.
You will have to add an audio cable with this cable as DVI is video only.

HDMI
"HIGH DEFINITION MULTIMEDIA INTERFACE"

USES:
This new cable connects High Definition or digital devices. It carries **both AUDIO AND VIDEO SIGNALS**. It will hook up HDTV tuner/receivers to TVs and is found on some high end DVD players.

LIMITATIONS:
The only limitations so far is that it's only for digital signals and can't help your traditional NTSC TV.

This cable will probably be pricey, but then you spent the money for the quality HDTV, you should budget for it...

BENEFITS:
This is a great cable. It not only carries High Definition video it carries AUDIO AS WELL! Plug and play. It can carry 8 channels of audio and still has spare room for more information. (This means that it won't get outdated quickly...we hope). So, it can handle all the video resolution it gets!

This cable sends a purely digital signal keeping all of the resolution and clarity of the source. There is no need for converting to analog and then back to digital for display. A much cleaner transfer results in "looking through a window" realistic images.

RECOMMENDATIONS:
If this connection is available on your TV and other equipment, **take advantage of it!**

You must match the cable to the connection. Remember: You cannot connect a DVI-A (analog) component to a DVI-D (digital) component. The configuration of the holes in the connection will tell you. (See the DVI connections illustration in the Connections chapter 3.)

DVI
"DIGITAL VISUAL INTERFACE"
COMMON NAMES: DVI-HDCP, DVI-D, DVI-I,

USES:
Sending either digital or converted analog signals from a high definition tuner, DVD, or Digital VHS to a high definition ready TV.

LIMITATIONS:
The DVI analog connection is not as good as the DVI digital. You must match the connections on your components and TV—a digital to digital or analog to analog. It carries only video and needs an audio connection to accompany it.

BENEFITS:
Using DVI-D, this cable sends a purely digital signal, keeping all of the resolution and clarity of the source. There is no need for converting to analog and then back to digital for display. A much cleaner transfer results in "looking through a window" realistic images.
Can handle all of the 1080 lines of resolution sent out used in high definition.

RECOMMENDATIONS:
Because these cables send digital signal, they can *cause* radio frequency or electromagnetic interference with your other analog cables. Other cables you use which have inadequate protection (shielding) may lose picture or sound quality . Be sure to use a high quality DVI cable that has good shielding to protect all of your cables from interference.

RGB-HV

COMMON NAMES:
"RGB CABLES WITH HORIZONTAL AND VERTICAL SYNC"
or "DB15 TO 5 BNC" OR "5RCA" OR "5BNC"

USES:
Used for hooking up a high definition tuner," set top box", to High Definition televisions that accept analog signals.

The end connector can vary. They can have RCA phono type ends, or they can be professional type BNC ends. Your local video accessory store carries adapters that will connect an RCA to a BNC or BNC to RCA depending on the terminals on your TV and high definition tuner. This cable can have 5 cables on both ends OR it can have a computer type pin connector on one end and 5 cables on the other.

LIMITATIONS:
These cables are still analog cables and as such are not as good as using a cable which can transfer a digital signal.

RECOMMENDATIONS
Use them when your High Definition hookup requires them. Choose a digital cable like DVI or HDMI if you have that connection available.

RGB/SVGA
COMMON NAMES:
HD15, D-SUB, VGA, XGA, COMPUTER MONITOR CABLE

USES:
Most common use is to hook up a computer to a TV so the TV can act as a monitor for the computer.

Found on projection TVs, plasma TVs, LCD TVs , DLP™ projection , and on occasion, rear projection TVs and Direct View CRTs.

LIMITATIONS:
This is an analog connection. It doesn't have as wide a band-width as DVI and it is not commonly used for connecting TV broadcast or other components other than computers.

BENEFITS:
Sometimes it's nice to use your large screen TV to display computer presentations or other computer needs.
Note: Use caution when displaying a computer's static image with rear projection or plasmas TVs. Burn-in can occur.
(See HDTV chapter 2, Burn-in.)

RECOMMENDATIONS:
Be sure to get gold connections if possible for best transfer of signal. Choose another connection and cable if available for high definition signals.

iEEE1394 cables may have 4 pins or 6 pins. Some will be 4 or 6 pins on both ends ("4/4" or "6/6") others will have 4 on one end and 6 on the other like the picture here above.

"IEEE1394"
COMMON NAMES: FIREWIRE, iLINK®, DTVLINK™

USES:
Some TVs and High Definition digital Cable TV boxes, Digital VHS, digital camcorders use iEEE1394. It is prevalent in computer use to hook up DVD burners, digital camcorders, external hard drives and more.

It is a fast connection that is bi-directional (lets the equipment send and receive information from the same connection, that is output and input in one).

LIMITATIONS:
HDMI and DVI seem to be the front runners in the digital connection race. HDMI has a much larger bandwidth (can carry more information) which may have more uses in the future.

BENEFITS:
It is a very fast, digital, (carries lots of information = great picture and sound). One cable/connection for both in and out for audio and video makes connecting easy.

RECOMMENDATIONS:
If you have it on two pieces of equipment with this connection you can use it without consideration. This is a great cable to hook up a digital camcorder.

Section 3: Picking the right audio cable for your connection

Basically, there are analog audio cables and digital audio cables. Analog audio cables carry stereo sound and basic Dolby Pro Logic® surround sound. Digital cables allow for digital surround sound like Dolby Digital® or DTS™(See HDTV chapter 2, "HDTV audio formats.")

Where analog sound runs on two cables, digital sound uses only one. Digital sound can be transferred along with video on cables like HDMI and iEEE1394. Using those connections, you do not need to connect a separate audio cable. With all other video cables (except an RF antenna cable) you will need to choose a connection and cable for the accompanying sound (unless you like silent movies!)

While analog cables use a separate cable for the right and left channel...

These photos show the difference in cables. These analog cables use braided wires and the optical digital uses a fiber optic cable

...digital cables can send the digital information down one cable to be translated by the receiver.

The transfer of digital signal is less likely to lose quality because of interference or other signal loss along the cable.

AUDIO CONNECTIONS

TYPE	IF YOU HAVE THIS CONNECTION.	USE THIS CABLE.	RECOMMENDATION:
RCA "LINE AUDIO" ANALOG			Use for analog sound. Can carry stereo, and matrixed surround sound like Dolby Pro Logic® and DTS™: Neo 6®
COAXIAL DIGITAL AUDIO			Choose this cable or the TosLink for digital surround sound. Carries full Dolby Digital® or DTS® surround sound. *You may need to also hook up RCA for stereo DVDs or broadcasts that are not sent out digitally.*
TOSLINK "OPTICAL" OR "FIBER OPTIC" DIGITAL AUDIO			Choose this cable or the coaxial audio cable for digital surround sound. Use Carries full Dolby Digital® or DTS® surround sound. *You may need to also hook up RCA for stereo DVDs or broadcasts that are not sent out digitally.*
IEEE1394 FOR DIGITAL AUDIO			This cable will only be used on high end a/v receivers with DVD-audio decoders. Most will use the 6 or 8 line audio to connect a DVD-Audio DVD player.
6 OR 8 CHANNEL LINE AUDIO			Use when you have a DVD player with a decoder and your receiver does not have that decoder, especially DVD-Audio, SACD, HDCD and with older a/v receivers that don't have digital surround sound decoders.

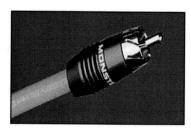

Some people have used an RCA video cable in place of a coaxial digital audio cable because they are theoretically built the same. Many experts claim that it doesn't have the same good quality of a coaxial audio cable designed for audio.

COAXIAL DIGITAL AUDIO

USES:
Connecting DVDs, High Definition Set Top boxes, and other digital sources to a Home Theater receiver.

WHAT IT IS:
This cable looks much like analog line cables. Inside, the cable is a coaxial cable with 75 ohm impedance (that is the same design as a video cable like the yellow RCA cable) and it uses an RCA phono connector. This copper cable runs digital sound information for all surround channels. When the information reaches the receiver, the speaker information is separated out and converted to analog for each speaker (they call that "discrete" information).

SHOULD YOU USE IT?:
If you want to get Dolby Digital® surround sound, your choice for digital sound is the coaxial or the TosLink optical cable. Some audiophiles believe the coaxial cable is superior to the optical cable. Most of us won't hear the difference.

RECOMMENDATIONS:
Use what connections you have on your equipment as your guide. When connecting many devices with digital audio (for example a DVD player and an HDTV receiver and a DVR and...) you may find you have a limited number of each type of digital audio inputs. You may choose one connection over the other to be sure you have enough of each type of connection.

If you are someone who likes to follow the advice of aficionados, this is your choice.

When you connect a TosLink cable, you can see the red laser light at the other end.

TosLink OPTICAL CABLE
COMMON NAMES:
DIGITAL AUDIO OPTICAL CABLE,
FIBER-OPTIC AUDIO CABLE

USES:
Connecting digital source devices like DVDs , High Definition set top boxes, Satellite receivers and other digital sources to a Home Theater receiver. Also used to connect out from your amplifier to a mini disc, CD or DVD recorder, devices that record digital sound.

WHAT IT IS:
Unlike all the other cables which send signal over metal (usually copper) wiring, the TosLink cable sends the sound signals as a light pulse. When you take the cover off the connection on your DVD or other device , you will see a red laser light shining. The plastic fiber allows this laser to travel to the input of your receiver.

LIMITATIONS:
Kinks in the cable will cause loss of signal. Be sure to wind it gently and buy a cable closest in length to the measured distance between connections.

BENEFITS:
See recommendations in previous section on Coaxial digital audio.

TosLink cables tend to be less expensive than coaxial.

TosLink, like RCA cables, got its name from its inventor. In this case Toshiba invented this cable.

"IEEE1394"
COMMON NAMES:
FIREWIRE, iLINK, DTVLINK™

USES:
Wait a minute, there's that cable with the letters and numbers again. This multi purpose digital cable can be used for audio only. Better home theater receivers are offering these "firewire" connections for use with DVD-Audio, SACD, and HD-DVD music formats.

WHAT IT IS:
It is a fast digital connection that is bi-directional (lets the equipment send and receive information from the same connection—output and input in one).

SHOULD YOU USE IT?
If you have a high end a/v home theater receiver and you have a DVD player with DVD-Audio, SACD or HD-DVD music formats, you may want to use a iEEE1394 cable to connect them. It sure beats hooking up a DVD players with 6 or 8 analog cables and the digital cable means less loss of signal.

RECOMMENDATIONS:
If you want to be surrounded by music, and plan to buy the CDs with this surround format, then use this cable if you have the connection.

LINE AUDIO
6 (OR 8) CHANNEL INPUTS

USES:

This sends digital signals which have been converted to analog audio signals to the A/V receiver. Some receivers are "digital ready" and don't have decoders built in, or some of the 6.1 or 7.1 channel surround sound (i.e. DTS-ES™) have the decoder in the DVD player and the receiver is merely capable of sending the sound to 6 or 8 speakers. These receivers cannot decode the digital code and must receive the audio signal already separated in the discrete channels and in analog form. Some music media is encoded with a surround sound like DVD Audio or SACD, and the decoder is built into the DVD player. Unless you have a new A/V receiver which will decode DVD-Audio and/or SACD, in order to play these discs, you will hook up each channel separately (Front Right and Front Left, Center, Surround Right and Surround Left and Surround Center Back or two surround center backs).

WHAT IT IS:

This is simply 6 (or 8) separate RCA audio cables that connect from a source that has converted its sound signal to separate channels before sending it off to the receiver/amplifier. You may remember that digital surround is 5.1 channels. There is a cable for the subwoofer information along with the other surround speakers making it 6 channels. (Likewise 8 channel is for 7.1 including 2 surround center back channels).

SHOULD YOU USE IT?

You are completely surrounded by sound and speakers and have a movie theater-like experience or an in-the-studio music experience.

RECOMMENDATIONS:

Unless your receiver has the decoder, you will need the analog hookups to receive the sound from your 6 speakers (5.1) or 7 speakers (with surround back (6.1) or 8 speakers (with 2 surround backs–8.1. Use only when required to for 6.1 or 7.1 channels , if you want DVD-Audio or SACD, or if you only have a digital ready receiver and built in decoder on your DVD. If you have a iEEE1394 connection, you will likely opt for that cable instead.

Speaker Wire and Connectors

Once you send that high quality sound to your receiver, don't forget the quality speaker cables to send the sound to the speakers.

Here, insulated cables, timed cables (the highs and the lows reach the speakers at the same time) and good connectors will insure that all the sound that the A/V receiver has received is passed on to the speakers. There are many quality cables that aren't the width of your finger. Some are even flat but have good construction. Like with interconnect cables, cheap flimsy cables will have signal loss and interference. Your best choice is to by better speaker wire instead of using speaker wire resembling the FM antenna wire!

You can connect bare ended speaker wire by twisting it around the peg of the speaker connector, or sticking it into spring loaded grips. By adding one of the connectors shown below it will be easier to connect and give you a better transfer of signal. Some people like to solder the connectors to the wires, or you can look for speaker connectors that are made to clamp on to the ends of the speaker cable without soldering (often labeled "no solder" cable ends).

TYPES OF SPEAKER CONNECTORS

Remember: you want a snug connection so there is no loss of signal.

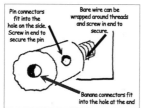   

| bare wire can be wound around a post speaker connection or poked into the side hole. | banana plug–will fit into the end of a post speaker connection | bent pin—can fit into the side hole of a post speaker connection or spring loaded speaker connection | spade–will fit under screw-type speaker connection. more common on older stereos |

Go to www.easier.tv to learn about how to hook up your subwoofer under "tip of the day."

Speaker wire can be flat and paintable, or thick . You may not need fat wire to get good sound. Check with your sales help or installer whether you need the behemoth wire.

When cutting your speaker cables, it's best to keep lengths of cables equal, even if one speaker is closer to the receiver than another.

SECTION 5: "UNLEASHED" Cutting the cord... "Wi-fi"
The new "Wireless" Televisions and Home Theaters

Let's face it, the thought of not having to deal with miles of cables is appealing. So is a flat screen on a wall with no unsightly wires; or rear speakers without running wires under the carpet or along the baseboards and up walls. Imagine a TV that you can take out on your deck and watch a DVD movie or the Olympics or catch up on your recorded "ER", while you are gardening. How about watching a movie trailer off the web before deciding which movie to see? Or a slide show of pictures from your computer to show Uncle Frank when he visits?

These are the benefits of "Wi-fi" (pronounced like "why fi"—a take off on the ol' "Hi-fi" term). Wi-fi is wireless technology with which a TV can receive information from a source without having to be hooked up to it. (It also refers to a wireless network of computers or wireless connection of computers to the web–think "wi-fi" cafes).

The picture sent to your TV can be from a DVD, your computer, the internet or any device hooked into an access point, or router (transmitter). The router receives the information from one of these sources and wirelessly transmits the information through radio frequencies (See section 1 of Getting the Picture chapter). The information is then received by another device, which is connected by cable to your TV. Or, it can be received by an internal wireless network card in specially equipped TVs. These TVs are usually equipped with special on screen menus that let you pick what you want to watch or listen to.

There are so many technologies for this: here are some...

For this wireless connection, you'll need a component that has the feature of networking with your computer. In this case, it is done wirelessly, but it can also be hard wired.

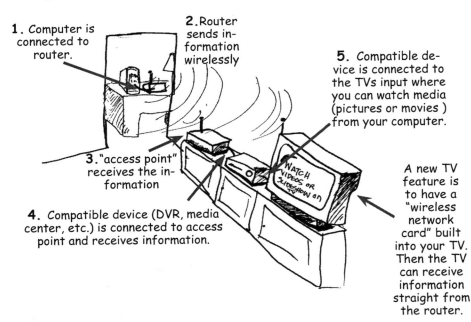

1. Computer is connected to router.

2. Router sends information wirelessly

3. "access point" receives the information

4. Compatible device (DVR, media center, etc.) is connected to access point and receives information.

5. Compatible device is connected to the TVs input where you can watch media (pictures or movies) from your computer.

A new TV feature is to have a "wireless network card" built into your TV. Then the TV can receive information straight from the router.

Remember that for a component to be part of the wireless network, it has to have the ability of being networked. It will either use an internal "wireless network card" or use the ethernet connection to attach to a wireless receiver. The product description and features will tell you if your product has networking capabilities.

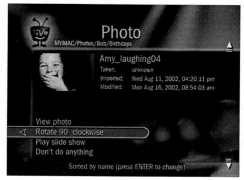

This TiVo® Series2™ hooks into a wireless network through a Wireless USB network adapter. Other networkable components may use an "ethernet" connection.

Wireless speakers, headphones, and some wireless TVs use RF (radio frequency) signals. They send the signal at the 900 MHz, 2.4 GHz or 5.6 GHz frequency like some portable phones. Be sure that you don't have interference from cordless phones, microwave ovens or wireless internet connections if you choose this kind of wireless technology.

This is a wireless transmitter and receiver
for home theater speakers
Photo courtesy of Kenwood

SECTION 6: Accessories for Cable Management

There are many accessories available today that can help keep wires from piling up behind your equipment. It is important to separate signal carrying cables from power cables to minimize signal interference from power cords.

Cable management can be as simple as twist ties or plastic ties (my friend uses covered ponytail rubber bands) to tie together cables into neat bundles. You can purchase special cable ties are which are made from Velcro and color coded.

Another option is flexible tubes that can be cut to the correct length. Some are made of fabric, others from plastic.

In the hookup chapter there is a section on furniture. Today's "TV stands" and "component cabinets" often have housing into which you thread your cables which keeps them together and out of sight. Look for this feature in dedicated home theater furniture and TV stands.

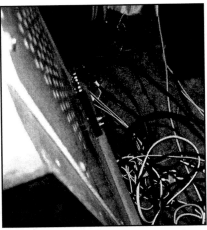

Without cable management

When you bundle your cables together, keep power cords separate from audio and video cables.

Keep cables in order with special cable ties and/or cable tubing...

Or you can hide them in the channels of special media furniture.

Hookup Planning and Preparation

WHAT YOU WILL LEARN IN CHAPTER 5...

-How to create a plan before you hook up your system.

-How hooking up through your home theater receiver or through your TV will affect how you control your system.

-Placement of your TV, components and surround sound speakers.

-How to pick furniture on which to put your equipment.

-What you will need in order to do the hook up.

Words to know in this chapter:

A/B SWITCHER
A/V RECEIVER
ANALOG SOUND
BI-POLAR SPEAKERS
BROWNOUT
BROWNOUT
PICTURE IN PICTURE
CENTER CHANNEL
CHANNEL
CHROMA
COMBINED SETUP
COMPONENT VIDEO
DEVICE
DIGITAL SOUND
DIGITAL SURROUND SOUND
DI-POLAR SPEAKERS
DUAL HOOKUPS OR
   DUAL CONNECTIONS
DVR
HOME THEATER
HOME THEATER RECEIVER
IN-LINE HOOKUP
INPUT
JACK
LFE
LUMINANCE
"MAGNETICALLY SHIELDED SPEAKERS"
OUTPUT
PASS-THROUGH

PICTURE IN PICTURE
PROLOGIC SURROUND
SOUND
RF CABLE
RF MODULATOR
RF REMOTE CONTROL
S-VIDEO
SHIELDED SPEAKERS
SIGNAL
SOURCE
SOURCE SELECTOR
SPLITTERS
STEREO
SUBWOOFER
SURGE
SURGE PROTECTOR
SURROUND SPEAKERS
SURROUND BACK
SPEAKERS
SURROUND BACK
SPEAKERS
SURROUND SOUND
TERMINAL
THX
UPCONVERSION
VIDEO SELECTOR
VIEWING ANGLE

WHY CAN'T I JUST FIND MATCHING CABLES AND STICK THEM TOGETHER?

1. You WILL get lost along the way

2. You will find it hard to use your equipment later and not know why

3. You will wonder why you spent money on any good components because now they don't look as good as they did in the store.

4. If you take it apart or add something, you will have to start from scratch.

"Oath of Easy Hookup"

I WILL TAKE ONE STEP AT A TIME WITHOUT SKIPPING AHEAD.

IF I GET CONFUSED AND FRUSTRATED, I WILL GO BACK AND REVIEW SECTIONS OR CHAPTERS I MIGHT HAVE SKIPPED.

I WILL DECIDE ON THE QUALITY I EXPECT FROM MY EQUIPMENT AND WILL BUDGET FOR AND BUY THOSE CABLES THAT WILL BRING OUT THE BEST IN MY SYSTEM.

I WILL NOT MAKE ASSUMPTIONS. I WILL DOUBLE-CHECK DIAGRAM EXAMPLES, ILLUSTRATIONS, AND REVIEW PAGES TO BE CLEAR BEFORE PROCEEDING.

I WILL BE DETERMINED AND SQUASH THE LITTLE VOICE THAT SAYS THAT THIS ISN'T MY THING OR I CAN'T DO IT...

I WILL CHOOSE CONNECTIONS THAT WILL MAKE IT EASY FOR EVERYONE IN THE FAMILY.

10 Steps for a successful hookup

1. Identify the connections on each component and make note of it on the "hookup worksheet".

Connections Chapter 3 will help you to identify types of jacks on your equipment. Note *all* connections.

2. Choose the source selector. Either your TV or Home Theater A/V receiver.

See "Choosing the Source Selector" in this chapter.

3. Choose your connections and which types of cables you will need..

In Cables chapter 4, see the video and audio charts for "Picking the right cable for your connection".

4. Play the "matching game". Be sure to note the number of cables you need and any accessories.

See "Play the Matching Game" in Section 5 of this chapter.

5. Choose where in the room you will put the TV, components, and speakers (for home theater.) Decide on which shelf each component will be placed.

See Section 7 of this chapter for more on equipment placement.

6. Measure for cable length. Measure distances between equipment jacks for cable lengths or measure distances between shelves (At the store, you can measure between the shelves of your chosen furniture at the store before bringing it home.)

See "Measuring for Cable Length". in this chapter.

7. Buy what you need. Don't forget accessories for cable management and stickers to label the cables and connections.

See Section 9 of this chapter, "Supplies and Accessories". Use shopping list form to help organize your needs.

8. Build furniture if needed. Put components in their places.

9. Gather together this book, your connections chart, a pen, dots, post-its, a flashlight, reading glasses, and wire strippers (helpful when cutting speaker wire). **Plan for more time than you think you'll need.**

See Section 10 of this chapter, "Hooking Up Your Equipment".

10. GET PSYCHED! Bring a sense of adventure and curiosity and a "why not try it?" attitude.

SECTION 1: Preparing to hook up your equipment...

The best thing you can do is plan your hookup before buying cables and making connections. The simple tips in this chapter can save you many headaches later and make the whole process of connecting your components a calm, fun, and easy task!

There are so many options when hooking up equipment that you could find yourself in the middle of your hookup, staring at dangling wires and asking yourself "Now, where am I supposed to connect this to?" Planning means that you have the right cables in the right lengths. Planning means that you won't have to return that TV you just bought because it doesn't fit in its space. Through planning, you will gain an understanding of how everything connects and how that will affect your later use and control your system.

PLANNING INVOLVES...

- **Discovering what you have**–An inventory of your equipment and its available connections.

- **Deciding how you'll hook connect your equipment.**

- **Deciding where you'll put your equipment**–which device needs to be placed near which other device, where is the optimum placement in the room, and where the speakers should be placed for surround sound.

- **Buying cables, supplies, and possibly furniture or new equipment.**

Planning means that you won't have to return that TV you just bought because it doesn't fit in its space.

Planning means that you have the right cables in the right lengths.

Section 2: "HOOKUP WORKSHEET" instructions

This will help you to choose your hookups and give you an idea of how each device will be connected to the next.

When exploring your connections, the following worksheet provides a place to note your findings. Seeing your inventory of connections on one page makes it easier to later decide how you will hook up your equipment.

How to fill out the Worksheet
(Read through all of the steps then come back and follow them.)

LIST *ALL* CONNECTIONS ON ONE PIECE OF EQUIPMENT THEN GO TO THE NEXT until **all** connections are listed as either an INPUT or OUTPUT.
(There are real world examples you can use for practice at the end of Connections, Chapter 3).

1. Look at your first component. Pick any one (or refer to the flow of the signal and determine the first component). Write down what it is (Cable TV box, VCR, TV etc.) in the INPUT column on the left and again on the same line in the OUTPUT column on the right.

2. Identify the connections referring to the connections chapter to identify the type of connection you find—RCA composite, RF, etc. List each group of INPUTS together both video and audio. (See example on next page.) Note how each are grouped and how they are labeled. (i.e.: Input 1, Video 1, Component 1, Ext. 1, etc.) An input or output group may offer a choice of video—"S-video" OR "RCA video" OR "Component Video". Note the choice by writing "OR" (See "TV vid 1" in example).

3. List all of the OUTPUTs on each device as you did for the inputs.

4. If you have more inputs than outputs, continue to skip lines so the next device name starts on the same line in the Input and Output column.

REMEMBER: EACH GROUPING IS FOR ONE DEVICE ONLY.
Though an input may have more than one video jack, (i.e. S-video plus RCA composite video), YOU MUST CHOOSE ONLY ONE!

BE COMPLETE. Double check that you have noted *EVERY CONNECTION* that you found on that device ***BEFORE MOVING TO THE NEXT.*** (Don't assume that you "don't need it now" or "don't want to use it now" and not write it down. You may change your mind and it will be confusing to add later.)

IMPORTANT! USE ONE SIDE OF A SHEET OF PAPER. You will later draw lines matching outputs and inputs. If you have more inputs than there are on the worksheet, use notebook paper. Tape a second sheet to the bottom of the first and draw a line vertically down the center labeling the left column "inputs" and right column "outputs".

You may also decide to do this on the computer in a spreadsheet or table. Doing this on computer allows you to move things around and add devices later without having to rewrite everything. If computers aren't your thing...you can always make copies of the worksheet page for future use.

WORKSHEET EXAMPLE

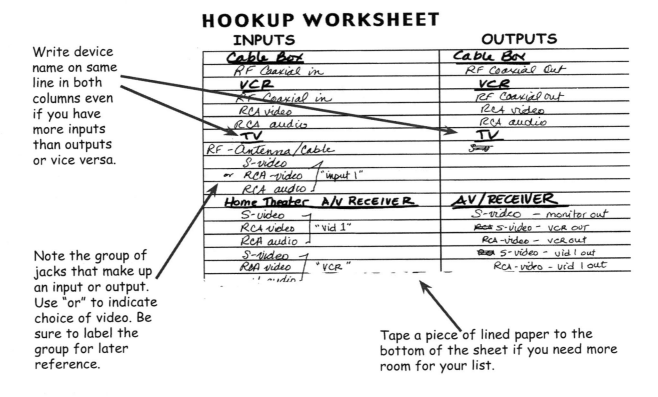

Write device name on same line in both columns even if you have more inputs than outputs or vice versa.

Note the group of jacks that make up an input or output. Use "or" to indicate choice of video. Be sure to label the group for later reference.

Tape a piece of lined paper to the bottom of the sheet if you need more room for your list.

HOOKUP WORKSHEET

INPUTS

OUTPUTS

You have a list of devices and their available inputs and outputs. How do you know which device hooks up to the next? You can start by knowing the logical flow of a signal...

THE FLOW OF THE SIGNAL (A REVIEW)

To get an idea of which devices you will want to connect, the following can give you a place to start. (You can understand more about signals by reading "Getting the Picture" Chapter 1.)

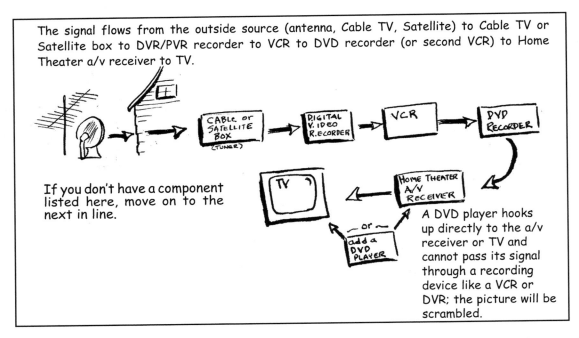

The signal flows from the outside source (antenna, Cable TV, Satellite) to Cable TV or Satellite box to DVR/PVR recorder to VCR to DVD recorder (or second VCR) to Home Theater a/v receiver to TV.

If you don't have a component listed here, move on to the next in line.

A DVD player hooks up directly to the a/v receiver or TV and cannot pass its signal through a recording device like a VCR or DVR; the picture will be scrambled.

Why did I choose this order? If you have digital Cable TV or Satellite TV, you will need it to go first into the Cable TV box or Satellite receiver for decoding and converting. If you want to record what you are watching on a DVR and archive old shows onto VHS, the DVR is then connected to a VCR. The DVD recorder is next for people who want to record their home movies from VHS to DVD. Sending the signal to the A/V receiver is used in the Home Theater Receiver-Based hookup.

While this illustration gives you a starting point in deciding which device to hook into the next, it is not definitive. It can be done other ways. Once you decide if your system will be TV based, Home Theater receiver based or a combination, you may decide to change things around. Also, you may want to use dual hookups.. Read on...

Section 3: Choosing the Source Selector for your system
How will you switch what you watch and listen to?

Whether you have a TV and a couple of components or you have a sophisticated home theater with an audio/video surround sound receiver, before you decide how to hook up your system and what you will need, you must choose what will direct the signal. Like a traffic cop, the system's source selector will control which source you watch and hear when you choose the input.

Your choice for source selector is TV based, A/V receiver based, or a combination. The easiest to use later is a single source selector, either the a/v receiver or your TV. On a TV based system, each component is connected to a different input on your TV. By pressing the corresponding input button on your TV or TV remote, the show you want is displayed on the screen.

With an a/v receiver, you will usually switch to a named source, like "VCR" or "DVD" that corresponds to the input where the device is connected. In an a/v receiver based system, all video and audio is switched to the input of the chosen component and the signal is sent out to the TV which displays what the a/v receiver sends. Typically you'll watch the picture on the TV and listen to the surround sound through your receive. You need only turn your TV on and off, the a/v receiver does the rest of the work. You can think of it this way: Changing the TV input tells the TV which of the input jacks to use, while changing the a/v receiver input switches which signal gets sent to the TV for display.

TV AS "SOURCE SELECTOR"

HOME THEATER RECEIVER AS "SOURCE SELECTOR"

How you switch to the device you want to watch, starts with how you connect your system.

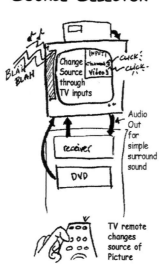

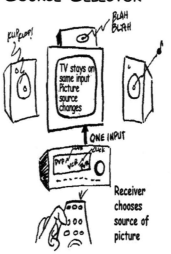

The easiest to use later is a single source selector, either your A/V receiver or your TV.

TV-Based System

With the TV based system, all devices, both audio and video are connected to the TV. If you want to listen to surround sound, you will connect the sound from the TV's audio OUTPUT to the a/v receiver's TV audio INPUT.

Note: you will only get digital surround sound if your TV has a digital audio output. This is almost exclusively found on HDTVs or HD ready TVs.

USE WHEN: You don't *have* an A/V receiver. Good for in-line hookups for bedrooms or 2nd TVs. Or, You mostly listen to sound through your TV's speakers. Or, some devices have video connections that you don't have on your a/v receiver. Or, your home theater a/v receiver only has Dolby Pro Logic® or stereo and not digital surround sound (or you have an HDTV with digital audio outputs and have sent the proper digital audio inputs into the TV).

BENEFITS: Simple hookup. Simple remote control switching between sources. You will change the input with the TV remote: (i.e. , from Channel 3 to Input 1,2, 3 or Video 1,2,3)

LIMITATIONS: Unless there is a digital audio output on your TV (only found on DTV sets), you will not be able to get 5.1 speaker digital surround sound.

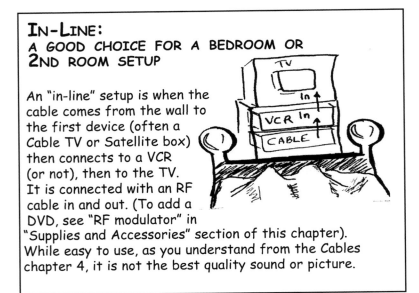

IN-LINE:
A GOOD CHOICE FOR A BEDROOM OR 2ND ROOM SETUP

An "in-line" setup is when the cable comes from the wall to the first device (often a Cable TV or Satellite box) then connects to a VCR (or not), then to the TV. It is connected with an RF cable in and out. (To add a DVD, see "RF modulator" in "Supplies and Accessories" section of this chapter). While easy to use, as you understand from the Cables chapter 4, it is not the best quality sound or picture.

All components connect into the TV. Optional audio out to the A/V receiver for surround sound.

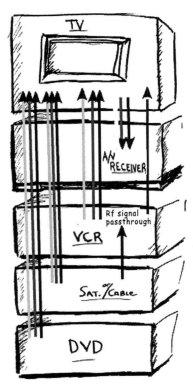

This illustration shows additional RF connection for VCR recording or easy viewing (be sure to check "Dual hookups" section for more information).

A/V receiver Based — (Home Theater)

Home theater, by definition, is when surround sound is added to your TV. But, in order to get the full surround sound experience you had to connect all of your components to the surround sound receiver. To make it simple, home theater receivers allow you to send both audio and video into the receiver (thus, "A/V receiver") so you can switch to what you wanted to hear and watch with one button. (See "Combined Setup" for further explanation).

USE WHEN: You have a home theater receiver and speakers, and want to listen to your movies or TV broadcasts with a sense of being in the middle of the action through your surround speakers. Or, if you have more components than you have inputs on your TV. Here both picture and sound are connected from the OUTPUTS of the component to INPUTS on the receiver. You will use the receiver to switch both audio and video at the same time by choosing what source you would like to watch/hear.

BENEFITS: Simple remote control switching with a single command. Great movie theater sound with a feeling of being in the middle of the action (have you watched "Survivor" in surround sound? You can hear birds in the surround sound speakers). The receiver can be placed in a components cabinet closer to other devices so you may save money buying shorter cables.

LIMITATIONS: Receivers can have many inputs and are overwhelming at first glance. Remember to take it slow. Also note that you may have to hook up more than one kind of cable. That is, some receivers cannot take an RCA composite video or S-Video input and send it out to the TV by a Component video output. (See "upconversion" in "dual hookups" in this chapter).

It may seem strange to send your video to the audio receiver but it will be easier to use later.

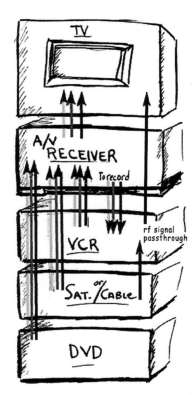

You may want to hook up the Satellite or Cable TV box to the TV through the antenna RF connection as a second hookup. Doing that will allow you to turn on the TV and use the volume like the good old days. There may be people in your home who are more comfortable with this way.

Combined Hookup : BOTH TV and A/V receiver

This hookup sends all of the video to the TV and the audio to the A/V receiver. While this seems to make the most sense, picture to the TV and sound to the surround sound receiver, it will be more difficult to use when you want to switch between watching a TV program to a DVD or other component. People with this kind of setup tend to have lots of remote controls and instructions on how to use them.

USE WHEN: Your receiver does not have "upconversion" (see "Dual Hookups" in this chapter), and you want to get the best quality picture or you would have to use more than one kind of output to connect to the TV. You have very high end video equipment that has video connections not found on your a/v receiver. Or, some people have trouble grasping the idea that the amplifier/receiver can switch VIDEO sources. They want video to go to the TV and audio to the receiver. Often, this is a hold-over because older amplifiers and receivers did not have video inputs and could not switch video.

BENEFITS: You may buy a few less cables with this connection. Direct video to TV erases the problem that you might lose picture quality when passing video signals through an a/v receiver. Chances are that if you have the desire to have this level of quality, you will want to research more sophisticated systems. If someone else has chosen this kind of hookup, you will need to work out how it will be easiest for all in your family to work the system.

LIMITATIONS: If you do a combined setup by running duplicate cables, it can get very costly. It is confusing now and confusing later. (See illustration next page.) If picture quality is important to you and you fear it might degrade if you put it through the receiver, then it's time to purchase a quality receiver to go with your taste.

The video is controlled by the TV while audio is controlled by the A/V receiver.

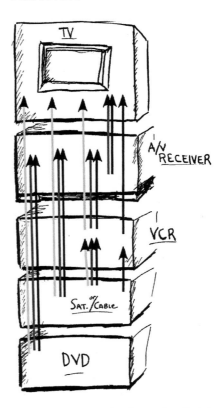

You may want to hook up the Satellite or Cable TV box to the TV through the antenna RF connection as a second hookup. Doing that will allow you to turn on the TV and use the volume like the good old days. There may be people in your home who are more comfortable with this way.

While using a combination hook up is straightforward to connect, later, you will need to use both the TV and A/V receiver remotes every time you change which source you want to view.

This is what often happens when you have a combination setup.

For example, to switch between a cable program and DVD:

You would need to change the TV to the input connected to the DVD to see the picture
AND
You would need to change the input source on the a/v receiver to the DVD to hear the sound.

This becomes particularly confusing when the inputs are labeled simply "video 1" or "input 1" rather than labeled "DVD" or "VCR", etc.

Uh Oh...
What if you have too many components and not enough inputs?

Solution 1: You can get a ***video selector*** accessory which takes inputs from many devices and has one output. (When you want to choose which device to watch, you switch the inputs on the selector. The input on the TV is unchanged.)

Solution 2: Consider stepping up to home theater. You will usually get more inputs on an a/v receiver than on a TV.

Solution 3: Have you considered it might be time for a new TV? If so, be sure you know the number and kinds of inputs you need now (list them) and consider extra for the future.

Section 4: Dual Hookups and other considerations

Mostly, connecting equipment is straightforward. The cable is connected to the output of the first device to the input of the second device. A single audio and video connection would normally be enough. There are times, however, when you'll want or need to connect with more than one video or audio cable from one device to another. Here are some of the occasions...

THE "GRANDMA'S CABLE" CONNECTION

For a home theater system, you will want to hook up your Satellite or Cable TV box for the best picture quality as well as for surround sound. What about the times when you don't want to listen to surround sound. Or, what about times when you have someone in your home who has trouble understanding that the sound is not coming from the TV and they get lost trying to adjust the volume? You can also connect the Satellite or Cable TV box directly to the TV through the antenna connection with an RF cable. This makes it possible to turn on the TV to channel 3 , to watch and listen to a TV program without turning on the receiver.

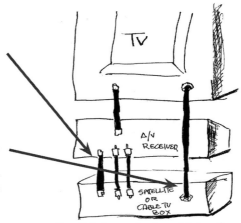

I call it "grandma's cable" referring to the traditional connection that allows you to turn on the TV get picture and sound without having to bother with the A/V receiver.

DON'T WANT TO LEAVE THE VCR POWERED "ON" ALL OF THE TIME?

VCRs allow the RF coaxial signal to pass through even when they are turned off. S-VHS VCRs can be set to pass-through a signal connected to the S-Video input and output.

 A standard VCR hooked up to its source –cable, Satellite, DVR–via the RCA jack will need to be powered on for the signal to pass through to the next component. If you don't want to always have your VCR turned on, connect both the RF coaxial antenna in and out, AND the RCA jacks.

OR choose to leave the VCR ON. Remember: Analog RF coaxial cables **Do not carry stereo signals**.

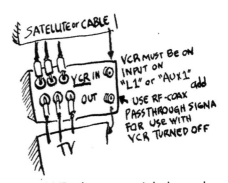

Some VCRs have special channel settings for incoming Satellite signals. If "line 1" or "aux" don't work, it's time to check the manual.

MATCHING QUALITY OF OUTPUTS TO QUALITY OF INPUTS

When connecting components to each other, it doesn't make sense to use a cable of higher quality than the one you will use to connect to your TV.

For example it's a waste of money to use a component cable for your DVD to your a/v receiver if you only have an S-video or RCA on your TV.

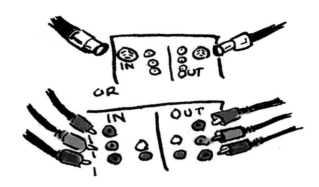

**MATCH THE QUALITY OF
CONNECTIONS THROUGH YOUR
COMPONENTS.**
(i.e., S-VIDEO IN, S-VIDEO OUT.)

UPCONVERSION OR DUAL HOOKUP ON A/V RECEIVERS

Different devices can use different types of connections to hook up to your A/V receiver. Perhaps your VCR connects with an RCA cable. Perhaps another device uses an S-Video. Your DVD will show its best picture through the component connection.

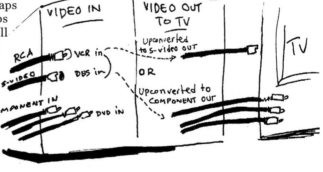

If your TV has a component connection, you'll want to connect the A/V receiver to the TV with the component cables. But if your receiver can't upconvert the signals from the RCA cable and the S-video cable, it won't be able to send those signals out to the TV. The RCA cable carries the chroma and luminance combined. The S-video separates the chroma and   luminance but doesn't further separate the colors like component cables do. The signal would have to be converted before it can be sent out. While upconversion is becoming available on more affordable models, you may still find two levels of upconversion. One can upconvert RCA signals to S-video. The other can upconvert all signals to component video out.

Without upconversion, you will need to connect the A/V receiver to the TV with cable types that match the inputs. Your A/V receiver's manual will tell you if you have upconversion or if you have to connect each type of cable. Instead, you may then choose to use a "combined hookup" rather than an "A/V receiver based" hookup, otherwise you could end up running double the video cables in then out of the receiver (and you would have even more confusion when changing inputs on the receiver and the TV).

If your receiver cannot upconvert the signals, *and* you have enough inputs on your TV, you may want to use a "combined hookup".

DUAL HOOKUP FOR DIGITAL AND ANALOG SOUND

Just last night I had to add analog sound cables to my Satellite output.

I listen to most of what comes from my Satellite with the receiver in Dolby Digital® surround which requires a digital audio cable. To record from my Satellite to my VCR, the VCR required an analog hookup as well.

Some a/v receivers cannot convert the digital sound signal to analog without inputting analog cables (stereo left and right). A VCR cannot accept digital information. When you hook up DVDs, Satellites and other devices with digital sound, connect **both** analog and digital sound cables to accommodate the analog devices that may record or play sound coming from the receiver like a VCR, a DVR, or a TV (if you are connecting sound it).

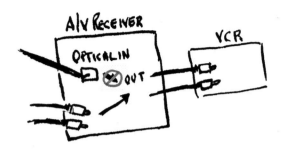

DUAL HOOKUP FOR PICTURE-IN-PICTURE

You may choose to connect your components **both** in-line with the other components, AND with a second connection to a TV input. This will allow you to use a "PIP source" (or "PIP input") button to switch between devices.

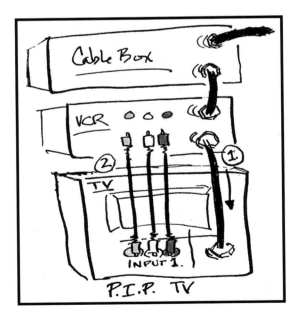

Section 5: Matching the Connections

WE'RE ALMOST READY TO PLAY THE MATCHING GAME...

✔ You've listed all your devices and all their connections on the input/output worksheet.

✔ You've decided the quality you want based on your budget and have an idea of which cables you want to use.

✔ You've looked over the "flow of the signal" illustration and determined which devices *you* own; you've considered which device the signal flows into first then out of, which second, etc.

✔ You have an idea if you want to use a TV-based, Home Theater based or Combined hookup. (You've checked your A/V receiver's manual and you know if it will upconvert the signals).

✔ You have looked at dual hookups and decided if you want a "grandma cable" or if you might need to hookup for both analog and digital audio. You've decided if you want to pass-through the signal through your VCR.

NEXT, MAKE A BOX SKETCH...

Using a blank piece of paper, draw boxes to represent each device and label the boxes. Use the "flow of the signal" to guide you where to draw the boxes. (When you start working with this, you may find that you want to re-draw the boxes to place one device in a different position closer to another...it's a process.)

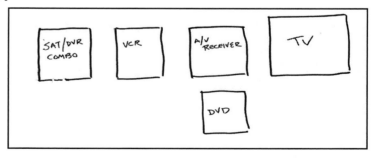

As you play the matching game, you will want to mark each step completed. You will be doing this by drawing a line from one device box to the next. (You may also want to draw a line from output to input columns on the worksheet.) Either way, I recommend that you **color code each type of cable** (i.e. yellow for RCA video, blue for digital audio, etc.) This will make it easy to see the number of which types of cables you will need. It will also make the drawings easier to read at a glance.

Write a number next to each connection as you go along. This will help you to follow steps during the actual hookup and will be an easy reference to label the cables and connections to keep track of where you are and to use as a reference if you ever have to reconnect.

Play the matching game

STEP 1. Start with the signal coming from the wall. Note a "**1**" next to the input of that device and write "from wall" (or "satellite" or "cable") on your box sketch and on your Hookup Worksheet. Your first device might be the cable or Satellite box. It could be your TV, VCR or DVR. Use the signal flow chart to help you decide which device to connect to first.

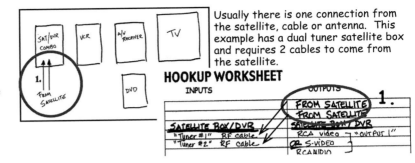

Usually there is one connection from the satellite, cable or antenna. This example has a dual tuner satellite box and requires 2 cables to come from the satellite.

STEP 2. On the Worksheet, find that same 1st device in the output column . Choose a type of audio and video output on the first device and match it to an audio and video input on the 2nd device of the same type (RF, RCA, S-Video & audio, Component & audio, etc.) If you find a group of audio and video together (i.e., "video 1"), use both the audio and video for that input group. (i.e., **not** video in from "video 1" and audio in from "video 3").

On the box sketch, draw lines representing the audio and video cables, connecting the first device to the second. Write a number "**2**" next to the connection you have just drawn.

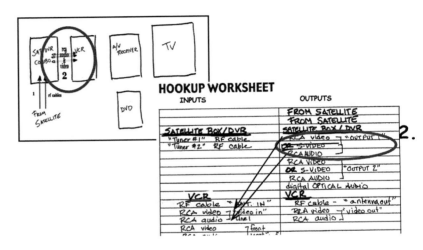

STEP 3. Finish matching all outputs from that device before moving on to the next device. If you want to do a dual connection or if you want to connect that device to another piece of equipment (i.e., connect the cable box to your VCR *and*, your TV or A/V receiver,) continue to draw lines for audio and video connections from that 2nd device to all equipment you want to connect it to. Give each new connection a new number. (You will use numbers to label cables and connections later.)

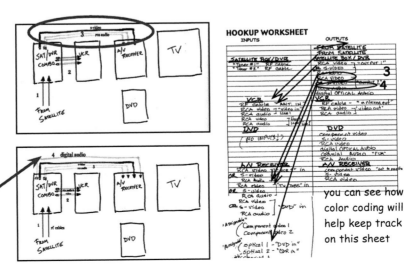

you can see how color coding will help keep track on this sheet

STEP 3. (continued)
Note that you could even have
a reason to connect one device
to 3 different other pieces of
equipment.

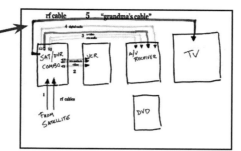

**Continue to draw lines
on your hookup sheet.**

**Though it sounds
confusing, it will make
sense to you as you
do it.**

STEP 4. Move on to the next
device. On the worksheet go to
the output column for that device
and match the outputs to inputs
of the next device in line.

Draw lines for the audio and video
connecting the 2nd device to the
next device.

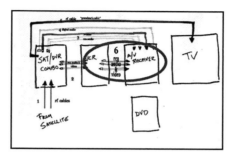

STEP 5. Decide on your
DVD connections. Draw lines
connecting the output of the DVD
to the A/V receiver (or to the
TV). *Remember to hook up both
analog and digital audio cables*
to an A/V receiver.
(In this example the A/V receiver
can only upconvert to S-Video.
I've chosen to connect the DVD
directly to the TV through
component cables.)

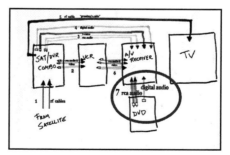

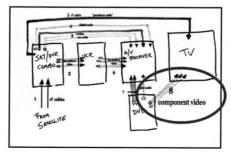

STEP 6. Choose the output to connect the A/V receiver to the TV. Even if you have a combined connection— where the video from all the devices connect directly to the TV— you will want to connect a video out from the A/V receiver if you have an "on screen menu."

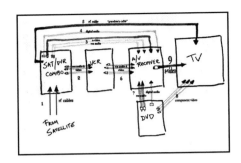

EXAMPLE OF COMPLETED BOX SKETCH:
HOME THEATER AS SOURCE SELECTOR
WITH COMBINATION SATELLITE/DVR

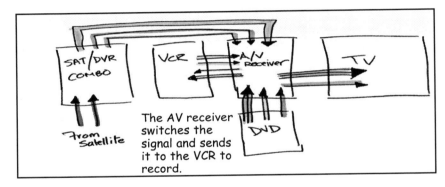

The AV receiver switches the signal and sends it to the VCR to record.

EXAMPLE OF COMPLETED BOX SKETCH:
TV AS SOURCE SELECTOR
WITH CABLE TV BOX AND STAND ALONE DVR

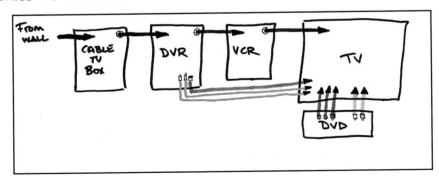

SECTION 6: Where will you put your equipment? Furniture and other considerations

Do you know where you will put your TV? Perhaps you already have a TV stand, cabinet, or media center. When you placed the components on the shelves did you first consider how they were hooked up? Is it in a way that you have the shortest, best quality cables? Do your remote(s) work well with all devices? (That is, you don't have to raise the remote above your head or lower it under the coffee table.) Is the component stand in a place that allows you to be comfortable while watching your TV and at a viewing angle that shows the best picture (for LCD TVs or Rear Projection TVs)? Can you set up surround sound if you want? Bottom line...ask yourself, "knowing what I know so far, am I happy with where my equipment is placed in the room?"

Whether you want to change the arrangement of your existing equipment or you need to purchase new furniture for your equipment, the following will help you to plan where you will put each component to optimize your hook up and viewing experience.

**You will want to decide where your equipment will go...
what kind of furniture, which shelf for each device and where in the room it will be placed in relation to where you will sit.**

Once you have made the box sketch, you can see which components need to be placed close to each other. Make a simple drawing of your media furniture. Draw an outline of the shelves on your unit and then referring to your box sketch, draw boxes deciding where you will place each component (like the drawings on the next page). If you haven't yet purchased your furniture, you may decide that a certain style (one where the components can be placed next to each other, like the one below right) may save you money by shortening the length of cables you will need. The savings from buying 3 foot component cables compared to 6 foot component cables (especially if you require more than one) will go a long way toward your furniture budget.

Once you decide which shelf each component will occupy, you can measure between the components to determine the length of cable you will need and note it on the chart. Record the quantity and length of each kind of cable on your shopping list.

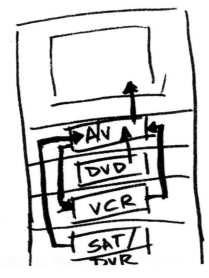

Using your box sketch as a guide, decide on which shelf each component will be placed.

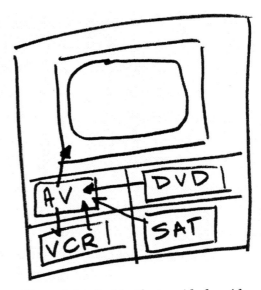

You might decide that a side by side style media center can aid your budget by requiring shorter cables.

Measuring for cables

You know where you will place the furniture that will hold your equipment. You have decided on which shelves to place each component to insure that more expensive cables will be shorter.

Many people believe that they can "eyeball" it and choose cables that are 3 feet or 6 feet, only to find that they have taut cables that can't be connected snugly. (Remember, a snug connection is important to get all of the signal information from one component to the next!)

WHEN MEASURING FOR CABLES...

Add extra cable length for hook up-you may need to turn or pull out the component and you'll need the slack.

Add extra cable length when you don't want a cable to stretch and show between side-by-side components (especially if on separate pieces of furniture). Measure down to the floor and then back up again.

When measuring for speaker cable, you will want to measure down to the floor (or ceiling if going through the attic), along the baseboard (or under the carpet or floor if you have crawl space) to the place of each speaker and then up to the height of the speaker on its stand or on the wall.

Measuring for speaker cable: front cable lengths should be the same regardless of the different distances from the receiver. (you can carefully coil extra length behind the speaker). This is true for the rear speakers as well. Use the longest measurement to determine length. (See "Speaker Placement later in this chapter".)

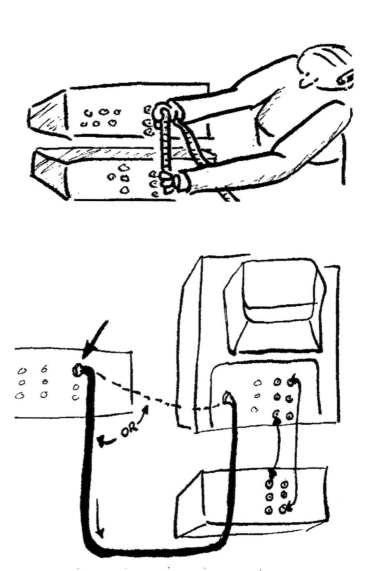

Purchasing furniture

Perhaps you are buying new equipment and want new furniture for your equipment. Perhaps you have a piece of furniture you would love to use for your equipment, like an armoire, and you wonder if you can make it work. Be sure that the furniture you plan to use for your system will accommodate it.

TO HELP YOU PLAN FOR PURCHASING FURNITURE OR FOR USING FURNITURE YOU HAVE...

1. What components do you own? How many? Be sure you have enough shelf openings. You may also want a shelf for a center speaker.

2. Will you need more shelves soon? (Remember DTV and HDTV will be here in 2006!)

3. Measure each component. (Typically, components are 17 inches wide but some have different "profiles"— they are different sizes).

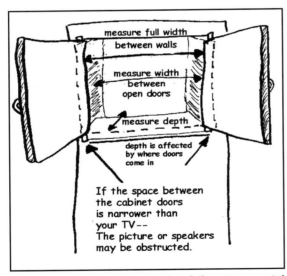

When measuring the width of furniture with doors, **BE SURE TO MEASURE WITH THE DOORS OPEN.** Measure the space **BETWEEN THE DOORS**, not just inside the cabinet. This will ensure that you can push your equipment into the cabinet.

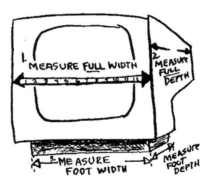

Be sure to measure the TV set completely! **Don't assume** A 27" TV IS 27" (It usually isn't...)

Measure the height, the width, and the depth, where it is largest. Also, measure the depth and width of the feet or base on which it stands.

You must measure the depth of the cabinet and the TV. If you want to close the doors on an armoire and the TV sticks out, it will always bother you.

If you love the armoire and it doesn't fit your TV, you can cut out a hole in the back.

When you are buying a new TV, and you have already bought the furniture for it...

Measure the TV to fit. This has often been a topic of disagreement among couples...one cares more about the TV, the other more about the furniture.

A TV that does not fit securely on the furniture could TIP OVER!

Consider the weight of your TV (especially larger CRT Direct View TVs). The weight is listed in the owners manual or, if you are buying a TV, you can ask about the weight. Media furniture will usually list the maximum size and maximum weight load if restricted.

DEDICATED FURNITURE AND MEDIA CENTERS

IS THE COST WORTH THE BENEFIT?

Dedicated media furniture (those made for your TV and components) may offer valuable features that simple shelving cannot. Good media furniture will give you access to the backs of the components, either by being open to the back or having backs that slide off or open when you need access. Many have discrete cable management systems—like hollow center support beams, through which you can thread your cables. Media furniture can have mounting brackets to accommodate flat screens and may be sturdier than simple shelving in order to accommodate heavier Direct View TVs. They may also have dedicated media drawers or cabinets to conveniently hold DVDs, CDs or VHS tapes.

Bottom line—if it fits your decor, and your budget, media furniture can make your life easier now and in the future.

Modular wall unit media centers can hold your equipment and be decorative. The downside to permanent or heavy structures is the inaccessibility to the backs of the equipment. This can make it difficult to add equipment, or remove equipment for repair. If you choose this system it is important to keep a note of how things are hooked up so that you can troubleshoot if needed.

Sliding backs allow accessibility to component jacks, and media drawers keep your DVDs, and tapes handy.

This is a channel to feed cables through keeping them neat and out of sight.

Photo courtesy of munari audio video furnishings and diamondcase designs.

SECTION 7: Placement in your Room— How to optimally arrange your room

Home theater rooms conjure up a picture of a darkened room with four padded walls, carpeting, and rows of theater seating.

More likely, your home entertainment will share a living room, family room or great room which adjoins a dining area or is open to hallways and other rooms. There may be partial walls and odd shaped rooms. How do you make the best of it? If you have home theater, be sure to read through both the TV and home theater sections before making your final decision.

The first consideration is placement of your TV.

Where does the cable come in from the wall? Do you want to inquire having it changed to better suit your needs? Call your Satellite or Cable TV company to find out what is required...

LIGHTING:
A darkened room, like a movie theater, is best for viewing. Direct light can wash out the color on your TV and lamps placed in front of a screen can cause glare and reflection. You also want to be careful of reducing the chance of glare reflecting from nearby windows. It would be better to place the TV on the wall with the windows behind it or have drapes that can be drawn to filter out direct light. Be careful that lamps in the room also do not create a bright glare on the screen when turned on in a dark room. Adjust the TV or lighting so they can live in harmony.

WALL OUTLETS—POWER, TELEPHONE, AND CABLE TV/SATELLITE/ANTENNA FEED:
You may want to consider necessary outlets when deciding which wall you will use. Ideally, there would be a power outlet nearby, a phone line (although a power outlet phone extension can work), and access to the signal coming in from outside. Outlets need not dictate where your equipment will go as there are many workarounds for distance problems.

The optimal viewing angle is within 30 degrees from center. Seating is at no more than 45 to 60 degree angle from the center of the TV screen.

TV Placement/ Viewing angle:

Sitting directly in front of the TV will, of course, be the optimal viewing angle. Here the picture will have the best contrast and brightness. To determine where to put additional seating use the illustration as a guide.

Viewing angle is most important with rear projection TVs or CRT Direct View TVs which do not have flat picture tubes. Older rear projection TVs have narrower viewing angles and is listed in the TV's owner's manual.

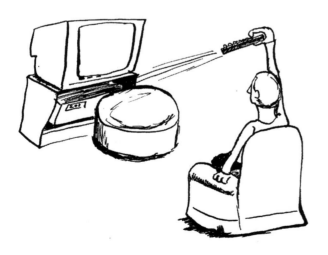

When planning your room consider other furniture, like a coffee table or ottoman, that might be in the way of the equipment receiving the signal from the remote.

If you are stuck with certain furniture arrangement, you can purchase a Radio Frequency (RF) remote that can be set up with your system. An RF remote does not need to be in line-of-sight with the device it is controlling. (It can even change channels from another room.) If you buy an RF remote later, your device will need to be attached to an RF antenna for the remote.

If you will have home theater surround sound, be sure to read through the next section before making your final decisions on TV and seating placement.

VIEWING DISTANCE—HOW FAR AWAY FROM THE TV SHOULD I SIT?

Other than our parents telling us that we will hurt our eyes because we were sitting too close to the TV, (actually sitting for hours close to the electromagnetic energy is not good for us), we now need to know "How far away will give me the best picture—or how big of a TV is good for the size of my room?"

In the 1940's, Otto Schade did research that concluded that the optimum distance for viewing at 330 line resolution TV (see HDTV chapter 2) is 7 times the height of the TV screen. Any closer and the lines become visible and the picture is fuzzier. Today's TVs have features that improve the picture quality and the rule of thumb is that a good viewing distance is 5 times the height of the TV screen. Remember that a 32 inch screen is 32 inches diagonally, so you will either need a tape measure, or you can use the handy chart on the next page.

That being said, if you are buying a new TV and you know where the seating will be in the room, measure (do not guess) the distance you plan to sit from the TV. AND BRING THAT TAPE MEASURE TO THE STORE. No, really! Take it from my years of experience...it is almost impossible to judge distances in an electronics store without measuring. Some people use their feet to judge distance but having a tape measure when you buy is essential as has been discussed—many good salespeople have tape measures as well.

While viewing distance is suggested when watching a Direct View CRT, for big screens, especially Rear Projection TVs, viewing distance is essential when watching any program that is NTSC resolution, standard TV.

Large screen Rear Projection TVs can look lined and grainy (can look pretty bad) when viewing a standard TV program. Moving back away from the TV will help.

VIEWING DISTANCE CHART

Use this chart to determine how far away from the TV you should sit or what size TV you should buy for your room.

Screen Size 4:3 square	Screen size- 16 x 9 widescreen	Optimal Viewing Distance
27 inch	33 inch	7 feet
32 inch	40 inch	8 feet
36 inch	44 inch	9 feet
40 inch	50 inch	10 feet
	55 inch	11 feet
	60 inch	12 feet
	64 inch	13 feet
	74 inch	14 feet
	84 inch	15 feet
Look for the closest sized screen on chart. Typically, 15 feet is good for a 60 inch or larger.		

EXCEPTION:
HDTV pictures can withstand close distances, particularly micropixel displays like DLP™ TVs, LCoS, and especially Plasma screens. (See HDTV chapter for descriptions of these TVs.) The rule for how far away to sit from an HDTV is a mere 3 times the HEIGHT of the screen. Remember, however, for the next couple of years you may be watching NTSC as well and you want to accommodate your distance for viewing standard programming.

SECTION 8: Arranging your room for surround sound

When making your final decisions of how to arrange your room, you will want to consider speaker placement as well as placement of the TV.

BASIC SPEAKER PLACEMENT FOR SURROUND SOUND INCLUDES:

Front speakers should be placed at least 6 feet apart.

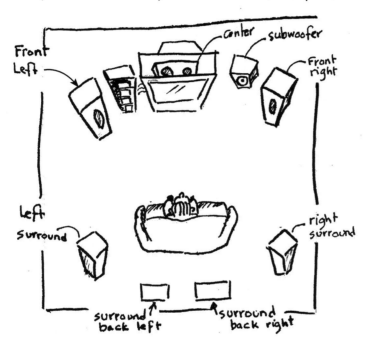

Center channel directly above or below the TV screen. If placed near a Direct View, CRT TV, it must be a magnetically shielded speaker or it will distort the picture.

Front Left and Right speakers at equal distance to the side of the TV and at least 6 feet apart .

Surround speakers to the side and slightly behind your seating area. And, if you have them. Additional back surround speakers should be placed behind the seating area.

Subwoofer—bass is non-directional. You will feel it more than hearing it. Put your subwoofer where it is convenient and where it won't rattle windows, walls or furniture.

ABOUT THX: Having the full theater experience like George Lucas intended when he created THX involves not only the equipment that is THX certified, but also room specifications and special speaker placement. If you spend the money for true THX, you should consider using a THX-certified professional installer. You may, however, benefit from THX speakers as they are "matched" to create sound well together.

OPTIMAL SURROUND SOUND

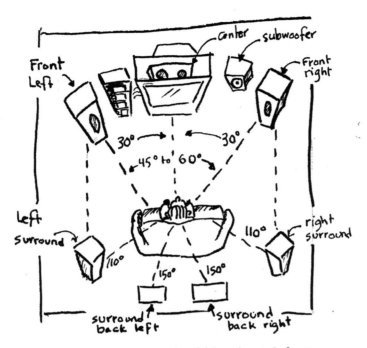

For **OPTIMAL** surround sound your speakers should be placed at particular angles.

For uniform surround sound, speakers should be at roughly the same height (which means that back speakers will be on speaker stands rather than on the wall).

The center channel speaker should be lined up with the front of the TV screen. Front Left and Right speakers slightly in front of the screen.

Optimally, your sitting area should be about 3 feet away from a wall.

Optimally, the center speaker should be at the same height from the floor as the front speakers. This illustration has the center speaker too high for optimal positioning.

Only use magnetically "shielded" speakers on top of or right next to your TV. The speaker magnets can cause an arc of purple or green discoloration near the speakers on a Direct View TV if not shielded.

Real-life Room Examples

Unless you are planning on creating a dedicated room for you home theater, you will probably find challenges in the room where you plan to have your home entertainment system. Doors, walkthroughs, windows, etc create challenges. The rule of thumb is to surround your viewing area with the sound.

You may have to run speaker wires along baseboards or under rugs. Paintable flat speaker wire is available and useful for running wires up walls. Speakers can be placed on speaker stands or mounted to a wall. When measuring for speaker wire, be sure to include the length of wire you will need to come up from the floor to reach the back of the speaker. Today there are wireless surround speaker options for home theater systems. If you choose in-wall speakers, you will want to have a professional installer who will use cables specific to this purpose.

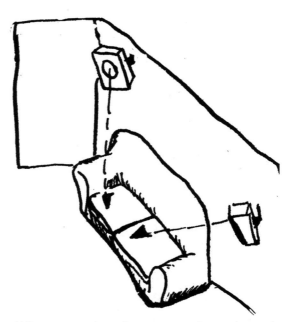

It is common in a smaller room that you will have to place your sofa against a wall. To achieve good surround sound, mount your speakers to the wall behind you (or on stands beside you if possible). Angle the speakers toward the center viewing area.

When mounting the surround speakers, be sure to keep them at least 1 foot from the corners.

Place the TV in the center of a wall if possible. If you have a fireplace, door or other architectural obstacle in the center of the wall, choose another wall.

In multi-use rooms like "great rooms", consider dedicating a corner to your home entertainment.

Rear speakers that are placed in the middle of the room can be placed on stands raising the speaker to 1-2 feet above your head.

Dipolar and Bipolar Speakers and Virtual Surround Speakers

If your salesperson suggests "dipolar speakers or bipolar speakers", should you use them? Understanding how they work will help you decide. Using regular surround speakers, sound is directed toward you. With direct sound you can pinpoint the location of a sound (like a door slam or footsteps, etc.) Bipolar and Dipolar speakers create an ambient sound; now the footsteps sound as though they are *in the room* with you.

Dipolar speakers have speakers on opposite sides. They are "out of phase," which means that the sound information to the speakers is delayed. This delay makes it seem as though the sound is coming from the side of the speaker (where there actually is no speaker). If you are sitting to the side of this speaker, it will appear it "fills the room" with non-directional sound; that is, you can't really point to where the sound is coming from.

Bipolar speakers are "in phase". Both speakers are going off at the same time. This allows sound to bounce off the walls of the room surrounding you with sound. By having the sound come from both speakers simultaneously, it gives you a sense that there are more speakers in the room. That the room is bigger, more like a movie theater.

Bipolar speakers might have speakers opposite each other or at a 45 degree angle.

Virtual surround speakers can be placed in the front of the room. These multiple long, "omni-directional" speakers also use a bouncing technique to "throw the sound" to various parts of the room.

While rooms with hall openings, doors or cathedral ceilings may make the set up challenging, the overall performance of a bipolar or dipolar speaker may give you less distorted sound than with a directional speaker. Check our website: www.home-electronics-survival.com for more information on these speakers.

BiPolar Speakers

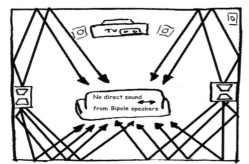

Bipolar speakers are set to bounce off walls to optimize the sense of being surrounded.

DiPolar Speakers

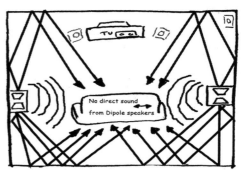

To get the most from dipolar surround speakers it is best to place them directly to the side of where you will be listening.

SECTION 9: Supplies and Accessories

In final preparation for your hookup, be sure to have the supplies and accessories you need.

Buy color coded dot stickers from an office supply store to help you stay organized. You can use these to label the cables and power cords in case you ever need to move your equipment or reconnect. The numbers on your worksheet can be used or you can write which devices the cables connect.

In the Cables chapter, review the options for cable management and decide on cable ties, tubes or alternatively on a media center which handles the cable management. (See "Dedicated Furniture and Media Centers" earlier in this chapter.)

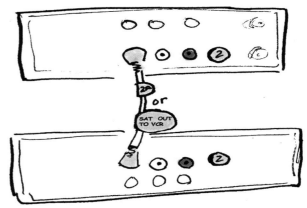

Place colored adhesive dots next to the connection on the back of devices and on the cable to be hooked into it. You can use either the number from your worksheet or write which devices it hooks up (i.e., "Sat out to VCR").

Video Accessories

You may have found that you don't have enough inputs, or the right kind of inputs, required for your components. To remedy the problem, you can purchase a number of video accessories at your local electronics retailer, or electronics accessory store.

VIDEO SELECTORS OR SWITCHERS: If you need more RCA composite video or S-Video connections than you have available on your TV, you can use a "video selector". These selectors can take the inputs from many devices and send the signal out through a single cable to one of your TV's inputs. When you use a switcher, you will change which component to watch by pressing the corresponding button on the switcher while your TV remains on the input to which the selector is connected. If you choose to use a video selector be aware that some offer a remote control option which switches between inputted components, saving you from having to walk over to the selector to manually change sources. Also, note selectors with S-video and be aware of dual connections.

A/B SWITCH: If you want to watch one basic Cable TV program while recording another, your can use an A/B switch. An A/B switch works similarly to a selector. With the A/B switch, two RF coaxial cables can be connected; one to the "A" and one to the "B". A single RF coaxial connection is then sent to the TV. Again, these are available with a remote control to save footsteps when you want to change from A to B.

An A/B switch gives you the choice of watching a signal coming out of your VCR into "A" (for example) or of watching basic Cable TV while your VCR is recording another channel. This is only available on analog Cable TV, not on digital Cable TV nor Satellite. Your TV must be able to use its tuner on the basic Cable TV signal (must be Cable TV ready and be set up for Cable TV (See chapter 1, "Tuner" section). *If you have an available RCA composite input on your TV, it is more convenient and better quality to connect your VCR through that input and basic Cable TV into the antenna input,* as this will eliminate the need for an A/B switch.

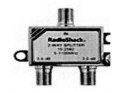

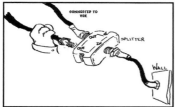

SPLITTERS: A splitter takes in a signal and sends it out to two (or more) destinations. When you hook up an A/B switch you will need a "splitter". The splitter is connected to the cable coming from the outside source (antenna or Cable TV) and is sent on to two components. In the case of Cable TV, it can be sent to a Cable TV box or VCR and the 2nd output to the TV.

Another common use for a splitter is to share the picture from a component (from a VCR or Cable TV or Satellite box, DVR or any component using an RF coaxial cable). In this case the split signal is sent to another TV, or a second VCR, etc. You will be watching the same channel on both TVs. Because there can be signal loss, choosing a quality splitter or one with a signal amplifier is preferred.

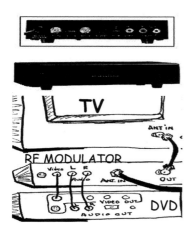

RF MODULATOR (ALSO CALLED VIDEO GAME OR DVD ADAPTERS): What happens if you want to use a new device which only has RCA line level connections or better? An older TV may only have an RF antenna jack which has worked fine for you until now. If you want to connect a DVD or a video game or a camcorder which don't have RF antenna jacks, you'll need a device called an RF modulator. More than just a difference in connection a modulator actually modifies signals to run on RF cables. The RF modulator takes in an RCA composite signal of up to 450 lines of resolution, and sends out a 330 line combined sound and picture to your RF antenna connection on your TV. For your convenience, many RF modulators have an RF pass-through to include your antenna.

Power Strips vs. Surge Protectors & Power Conditioners

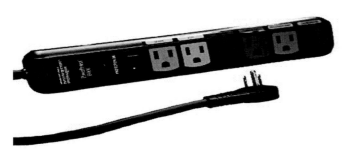

PROTECT YOUR EQUIPMENT!!
All electronics run on electricity. If power was always running at a steady level everything would be fine. Power is called an electrical *current*. If you think of the distance power must travel from power plants and distribution centers, there is a constant ebb and flow in the electrical current. Sometimes the power current will spike up- - "**SURGE**"–, sometimes it will diminish-- a "**BROWNOUT**". Too much power from a surge can run through computer chips that are used in audio amplifiers, TV picture processing, or an array of other features. The surging power is too much for the delicate chips and even small surges will result in a loss in quality now and shorten the longevity of a component. This is often what has happened when you have an intermittent or undetectable problem with your equipment or its life has been shortened. Big surges, like a lightning strike, can *fry* your component, rendering it unusable. A brownout is unable to provide the power needed to run a high powered piece of equipment so quality of sound or picture suffers and there will usually be a surge of current before the electricity reaches a normal range.

This is why a quality **SURGE PROTECTOR** is **REQUIRED** for every piece of equipment that uses electrical power (that would be all of them). Surge protectors are **NOT the same as INEXPENSIVE POWER STRIPS** with multiple outlets which simply give you more room to plug things and an extension cord to a wall socket. Look for surge protectors with an equipment guarantee. This will pay for any equipment connected to the surge protector in the event of a damaging power surge. Surges can come through any wires connected to equipment. Cables and Telephone cables run on an electrical current and can carry damaging surges in to your equipment. It's a good idea to buy a surge protector with telephone and cable connections. When hooking up, you will simply run the cable and telephone lines from the wall to the surge protector and then out again, as if you were just hooking it

up from the wall. Lastly, be aware that a large surge can render a surge protector useless. A very large surge will FRY the surge protector. (It sacrifices its life to save your equipment— noble little guy.) Many small surges can also burn out a protector. If the surge protection indicator on the strip light is no longer lit, it may be time to replace it.

POWER CONDITIONERS

IF YOU OWN HIGH END EQUIPMENT, ESPECIALLY HDTV, consider purchasing a power conditioner. Power conditioners can provide enough power, without interference to your high end audio and video. A/V receivers and amplifiers, and TVs require more power than other components. By hogging more power, they can diminish the quality of picture and sound from your other components connected to the same surge protector. Power conditioners, and some high end surge protectors typically feature high current outlets that provide more power to TVs and amplifiers or a/v receivers without sacrificing the power to other components. You will want to follow the labels to plug in the equipment labeled for each outlet. Also, the power in your home can gather interference from other appliances on the same circuit (like a washing machine, air conditioner or refrigerator) power conditioners diminish that interference.

A power conditioner "cleans" the power, blocking and reducing electronic noise causing interference that result in humming sounds or picture static (sometimes called "mosquitoes"). If you paid for quality equipment, you will want to invest in a power conditioner to see and hear the quality which you expect from your high end components.

All photos of surge protectors and power conditioners by Monster Cable Products, Inc.

SECTION 10: HOOKING UP YOUR EQUIPMENT!!!

ARE YOU READY TO START HOOKING UP YOUR EQUIPMENT?

✔ You have listed all of your equipment connections on your hookup worksheet.

✔ You have matched the connections and drawn a box sketch numbering each set of connections you will use, and color coding the different types of cables. (You know if your A/V receiver can upconvert to component video or S-Video and you planned accordingly.)

✔ You have decided where to put your equipment—both where in the room and on which shelf. You've purchased and assembled any furniture and rearranged your room. For cabinets and other furniture, you have holes to run cables and power cords from equipment.

✔ You have measured and purchased your cables, accessories and power conditioner or surge protector.

✔ You have purchased or gathered stickers, cable ties or other cable management.

DO YOU HAVE EVERYTHING YOU NEED?

❏ **TV and equipment**
❏ **Owners manuals** — don't panic, they're for reference in a pinch.
❏ **All cables and accessories.**
❏ **Dot stickers**—for labeling cables and connections.
❏ **Small sticky pads**—you'll be labeling cable packages.
❏ **Pen**—for marking dots, sticky labels, and checking off your box sketch as you complete each connection.
❏ **Paper**—you never know when you need to write yourself a note.
❏ **FLASHLIGHT**—any kind that can stand by itself is helpful. Hiking flashlights on headbands work great!
❏ **Your box sketch and Hookup worksheet**—essential.
❏ **This book**—it may help to look at the cables and connections chapters for tips of how to connect certain cables.
❏ **Wire stripper and cutter** *if you are connecting speakers.* There's a handy all-in-one tool or you can use a sharp knife to carve off the plastic around the speaker wire and sharp scissors for all but very fat cables.
❏ **A friend or helper — recommended** for placing or moving heavy equipment or to hold the flashlight.
❏ **Media** to test your equipment--DVD. CD, VHS tape etc.

HOOK IT UP! STEP BY STEP

1. **Put the equipment in place--** if you cannot get behind the furniture or the reach the back jack panel, turn the devices sideways. If you are using a media center that could be moved without the TV, be sure you can reach the backs of the equipment, connect the available pieces then move the stand into its final place before putting the TV on the stand.

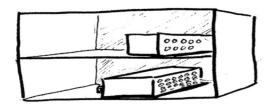

If the back panels will be blocked when equipment is in place, turn your devices sideways.

2. **Put speakers in place** (you may not want to mount them until you have listened to them in place). If you are pretty certain of where you place the speakers, cut speaker cable to fit the distance. If you are running cables under the house or through the attic, you may need to drill a hole in the floor or ceiling to bring the cables in. If you must run the cables around the room, you will probably want to measure along the baseboards. Do not secure wires with screws or pull up carpeting until you have listened to them and are sure that it sounds the way you want.

The front right and left speaker cables should be of equal length. This means both cables should be the length that will reach the speaker furthest from the receiver. This is true for the surround right and left speakers too.

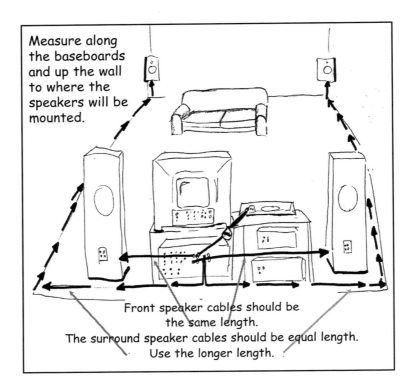

Measure along the baseboards and up the wall to where the speakers will be mounted.

Front speaker cables should be the same length.
The surround speaker cables should be equal length.
Use the longer length.

3. **Label the cables' packaging** --using your box sketch as a reference, gather all of the cables and put sticky notes on the packages. On the sticky notes, write what they connect: VCR to TV, or DVD to A/V, etc. Sort cables into separate piles for each device so you can go to that pile when you hook up that device.

4. **Connect! Label connections and cables as you go!** *Choose a dot color for audio, for video, and for both* (like RF cables and hdmi). By doing this, you can quickly recognize if it's audio or video and you can match numbers (#3 audio and #3 video).

Start with the cable coming from the wall—even if it has already been connected. On 2 dots, write a "# **1**" and "wall to Sat" (or "wall to cable"). Stick the dot next to the input on the Cable TV or Satellite box. Fold the dot in half around the cable that is coming from the wall (use the same color dot). Now connect the cable.

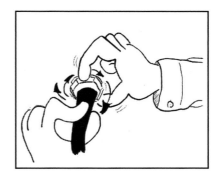

On your box sketch, place a check mark next to the connection you just made and move on to #2.

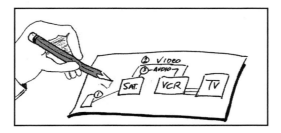

If you are connecting the box to the next device with the RF cable or other combined audio and video cable, follow the next directions with only one cable:

5. Write a "**#2**" on **3** video colored dots. Place the first dot on the device next to the #2 output connection, per your box sketch. Put another dot at the other end —next to the input of the next device. And put the third dot on the cable. Write a "**#3**" on **3** audio dots for the audio that goes with the video, and repeat. Connect the cables. On your box sketch, check off the connection you just made and repeat for the next connection on the sketch.

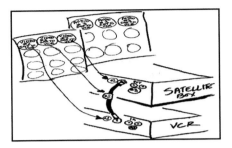

6. **Continue until you have connected all outputs from the first device to the second device** (or to the TV and/or the A/V receiver). Use the dots to label each connection. Connect the cable. Check off the connection on your box sketch and move to the next connection until all outputs are completed for that device.

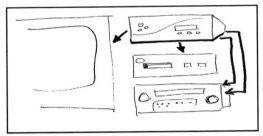

Check your pile of cables to ensure that you have used all the cables for that device. If you have cables left over and you are sure you have connected both audio and video (or audio and video combined), review the box sketch noting that all outputs have been checked off. If so, put the extra cables aside for now...you may have mislabeled them and will need them for later. Be sure to *open cable packaging **only as you use them.*** This helps you to keep track of them so there aren't stray, unlabeled cables laying around. (Also if you miscalculated your number of cables, you can return the unopened packages.)

Pay attention that each cable is pushed in completely and makes a snug connection. With equipment that has to be turned or pushed back into place, this is especially important so that it doesn't disconnect itself after you have move it.

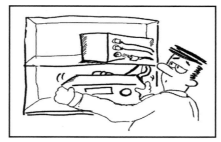

Be sure that the pins and holes are lined up correctly, before pushing in pin connectors like S-Video, hdmi or dvi, or TosLink optical audio. (See tips in Cables and Connections chapters.) *Don't force the connection!!* A pin can brake off and ruin the cable; worse, the pin could become broken and lodged in the device input.

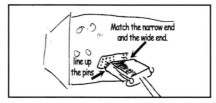

As you connect cables, try to run audio and video cables separate from power cables. Plastic cable tubing or cable ties helps keep signal carrying cables away from the interference of electrical power. (See cable accessories in chapter 4).

Be sure cables aren't squeezed, pinched or bent at right angles. It can interrupt transfer of the video or audio signals. Instead wind up excess cables into loose circles and secure with a cable tie (or twist tie or plastic tie).

Speakers

7. Prepare the cables to connect them to the speaker connections if you are connecting speakers to an A/V receiver. (See the speaker wire connectors section of the cables chapter.)

Start by using a sharp knife or wire stripper to remove the plastic outer cover from the speaker wire, about 1 inch.

For wire strippers, place the cable into a hole which corresponds to the size of the cable, squeeze the stripper together and pull off the plastic.

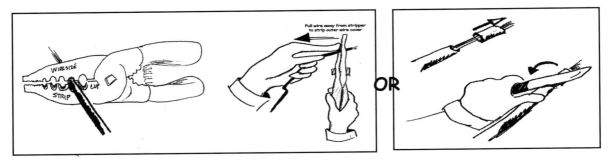

Or, using a knife carefully cut through the plastic outer cover to the wires, gently slicing completely around.

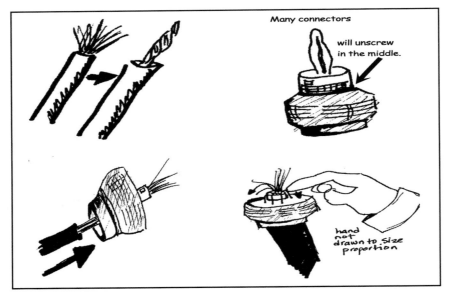

Twist together the exposed wire. You will want to put on the cable connectors and connect the speakers. Some connectors use solder to be connected, others will crimp on to the wires, still others will be unscrewed and flayed. See the illustration.

8. **Connect the speaker cables to the receiver and speakers**. You will still want to listen to them before you do any final mounting or securing speaker cables to walls, under rugs or other permanent work.

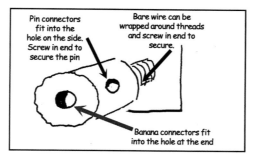

Testing --Does it work?

9. **Plug the power of all devices into your surge protector**. (See earlier in this chapter on power to find out why you should be using a surge protector.) *It can be helpful to label the plugs with the name of the device.* Use your colored dots or power cable labels that come with your surge protector. This way, if you later need to unplug a device you don't have to follow each plug to determine which one you want. If using a labeled, home theater power conditioner, make sure to plug your TV into the TV outlet and your a/v receiver into its spot. These outlets direct more power to these high powered devices.

10. As you start testing devices, you may be required to set up the TV or other equipment. You may have to tell the TV if you have Cable TV/Satellite or an antenna. You may have to assign inputs on HDTVs or a/v receivers. If you get a setup screen when you turn on a device, or if you do not receive a picture, check the manual for initial setup of your TV or device.

FOR TV BASED CONNECTIONS:

Now turn on the TV. Start with your Satellite or Cable TV box. If you have connected the box with an RF cable, be sure the TV is on channel "3" (or 4 if your area requires it). *Be sure you can see the picture, that there is no interference and that you have sound.*

If you have connected the Cable TV or Satellite box to the TV with RCA or other cables, press the input button on your remote until you reach the input you used, (i.e., video 1, 2, 3, etc.) You should have it noted, but if you don't, just keep pressing the button to go through the inputs. Note: your button could also be labeled Source or TV/video (**not** TV/VTR). (If you do not have a satellite or Cable TV box, and you connect directly to the TV, turn on the TV and start changing channels on the TV's tuner.)

TV-Based

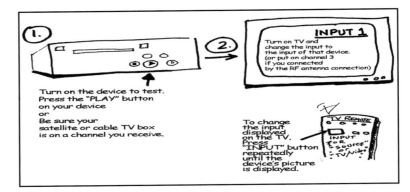

FOR A/V BASED CONNECTIONS:

Turn on your a/v receiver. Now, using the remote, choose the "source" on the a/v receiver. (This is why it was important to note the label on the input connection when you first listed the connections.) It may be TV/DBS (stands for "Digital Broadcast Satellite") or something else. Change the TV to the input to which the a/v receiver is connected by pressing the input button   See that the TV is getting the correct picture signal.

A/V receiver Based—Home Theater

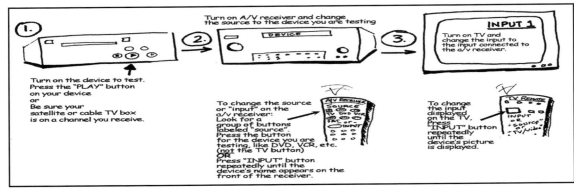

Make sure you hear sound out of all of your speakers which means you may want to walk around the room and put your ear up to each speaker—it's best to listen to a movie or show you know has surround sound.

FOR COMBINED SETUPS where you are using an A/V receiver for sound, turn it on too: (Again, you may have connected the Cable TV or Satellite box to the TV with an RF cable, if so, put your TV on channel 3 and you will hear sound from your TV set.) Otherwise,
Change the TV to the input to which the cable or Satellite box is connected. (See previous step). Now, using the remote, choose the "source" on the A/V receiver. (This is why it was important to note the label on the input connection when you first listed the connections). It may be TV/DBS (stands for "digital broadcast Satellite") or something else.

COMBINED—USING BOTH TV AND A/V RECEIVER

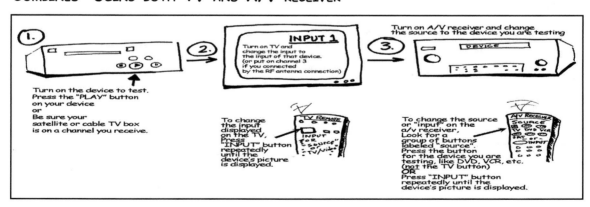

11. Continue to check all devices...

Put in a DVD into the player, a VHS tape into the VCR, etc. and press "play" on the device. Change to the input on the TV and/or the A/V receiver as you did to test the Cable TV or Satellite. Check picture and sound.

Once you determine that you have picture and sound from each device, you can put on the final touch. Mount speakers and secure speaker cable. Move furniture or devices into their final place. Put on media cabinet doors, shelving backs, etc. Only optimize picture and sound once all devices have been put into their final places.

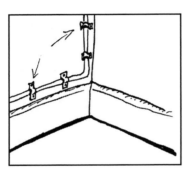

SHOPPING LIST
EQUIPMENT: (CIRCLE WHAT YOU NEED)

TV   DVD   VCR   DVR   SATELLITE   DVD-R

HOME THEATER RECEIVER   HDTV SET TOP BOX   HOME MEDIA CENTER

NEEDED CABLES:

Quantity	Type of Cable	Length of Cable	Quality Desired

ACCESSORIES NEEDED: ADAPTORS, RF MODULATORS, SWITCHERS, SPLITTERS, ANTENNA, etc.: _____ _____ _____

FURNITURE: # OF SHELVES _____

TV MEASUREMENTS: ____HEIGHT ____WIDTH ____DEPTH;
____WIDTH OF FEET; _____DEPTH OF FEET (SEE MEASURING SECTION.)

ON EVERYONE'S LIST:
- SURGE PROTECTOR OR POWER CONDITIONER (SEE PREVIOUS SECTION)
- COLORED DOTS FROM OFFICE SUPPLY STORE
- CABLE MANAGEMENT SUPPLIES (TIES OR TUBES) (FROM HOME STORE, OR ELECTRONICS STORE)

NOTES:

GLOSSARY

MAKING SENSE OF THE JARGON
DEFINITIONS FOR TECHNICAL TERMS...

GLOSSARY

2.4 GHZ: This is 2.4 gigahertz. A radio frequency at which many devices broadcast their wireless signal. It could be a portable phone, wireless surround speakers or even your wireless computer network.

3:2 PULLDOWN: (ALSO CALLED 2:3 PULLDOWN): film movies run at 24 frames per second (see "fps"). Videotape (like TV and camcorders) run at 30 frames per second. In order to have a smooth picture, it is best to convert the film movie from 24 to 30 frames per second. This added feature on TVs and devices is done through a computer processor in the TV or device.

5.1 CHANNEL SURROUND SOUND": Audio that "surrounds" you, using 5 speakers and a low frequency effects channel (subwoofer that plays the booming lows or "bass"). The five channels are Left and right front, center channel, and surround right and surround left. The subwoofer is given .1 status.

802.11 (802.11a, 802.11b, 802.11g, 802.11n): This is the frequency used by wireless computer routers to connect computer networks without cables. For wireless, a device must have a receiver (like a wireless "card". 802.11 is also being used in audio and video devices to wirelessly send picture or sound to another device).

900 MHz: A radio frequency at which many devices broadcast their wireless signal. It could be a portable phone, stereo headphones or even a wireless TV.

A/B SWITCHER: An accessory used when you want to connect 2 devices to a TV with only one antenna (RF or coaxial) input. Often used with a Cable TV box and VCR. "A/B" refers to the switch between device connected to "A" and device connected to "B". There is usually a physical switch. This switch lets the signal from the chosen device to be sent to the TV. Because most TVs now have more than one input, there is less of a need for this accessory.

A/V RECEIVER: "Audio/Video" receiver. This is the component that amplifies the sound to be played through your speakers. Similar to a stereo receiver, in that it often has a radio "tuner" and can connect to a variety of audio components, the A/V receiver also accepts video components and the video signals from those components. This gives you the convenience of switching the input on one device rather than having to switch the video on the TV and the audio on the receiver. A/V receivers are at least surround sound receivers and are also called "home heater receivers."

AC-3: "Audio coding 3" the original name for digital surround sound used in Home Theater. Usually it is 5.1 channel with 3 speakers in front (a left, center, and right), and 2 in back of you (surround left and surround right). The ".1" refers to the subwoofer which reproduces low frequency (bass) signals. See HDTV chapter 2 for more on digital surround sound.

ARTIFACTS: Interference in a digital picture. Usually used to refer to the boxy shapes that appear in dark areas of the TV picture or in fast moving scenes. Better TVs and DVDs have chips and processors to reduce the occurrence of artifacts. See "Line Doublers/Scalers" in HDTV chapter 2 for more information.

ASPECT RATIO: A number read as a ratio that describes the shape of a TV picture. The aspect ratio for NTSC, traditional square shaped picture is 4:3; the shape of a letterbox picture is 16x9. Widescreen pictures that retain the shape of the original movie shown in a movie theater has yet another ratio (wider and not as tall) and cinema wide has yet another.

ASSIGNABLE INPUT: Found on a/v receivers; there are a number of digital audio inputs (coaxial and/ or optical audio) or component video inputs that are not dedicated to any particular component. You can "assign" a particular device to use that input. This is typically done in the a/v receiver's set up menu.

ATSC: "Advanced Television Standards Committee". This is digital TV including HDTV. It is the future TV standard that is set to insure that all broadcasters will send a signal and televisions and other atsc tuners can receive. NTSC is the analog standard we will soon be leaving behind, the standard of your current TV unless you have purchased an HD ready, HDTV or other digital TV.

BAND: a range of radio frequencies over which picture and sound can be sent and received. The UHF band is made up of the channels above channel 13. See Chapter 1.

BETAMAX ACT: The supreme court decision which stated that a private citizen has the right to copy movies and TV programs for personal use. See HDTV Chapter 2.

BI-DIRECTIONAL: A connection or cable capable of sending *and* receiving signals between devices. A bi-directional connection serves both as an input and output. iEEE1394 or firewire is an example of bi-directional cable.

BIPOLAR SPEAKERS: Speakers commonly used as surround sound rear speakers. There are two speakers in the speaker cabinet that create sound that bounces off nearby walls giving the listener a sense of being "surrounded" by non-directional sound.

BITSTREAM: flow of digital data. (Literally a stream of "bits" of digital information) some digital audio connections are labeled "bitstream"

BNC: "Bayonet Neill Councelman" connection (you will probably *never* hear it called that); these are professional connections that have found their way onto some HDTV monitors and HDTV tuner set top boxes. Because these connections lock on, they have a superior ability to transfer video signals. See Connections chapter 3 for pictures of BNC connectors.

BNC CONNECTORS: See "BNC". The professional video connectors that turn to lock onto a BNC terminal. You can get adaptors to change an RCA phono connector to BNC and vice versa.

BROWNOUT: Refers to the electrical power current coming into your home. The amount of power is inconsistent and when the amount of power dips, it can cause dimming of lights or less quality in sound and picture from your home entertainment devices. The most important thing to know about brownouts, is that the power spikes (surges in) before it settles to around normal. These spikes can damage your equipment permanently. This is why it is important for all electronics to be connected to a surge protector.

BURN-IN: A faint, permanent ghostlike image of a static scene that is caused by pixels showing the same color or intensity for periods of time. Burn-in is most common on Rear Projection televisions, and is a problem being solved on Plasma TVs. To avoid burn-in, never leave a static image like a DVD menu, static backgrounds on video games, computer desktops, constant stock tickers, nor black bars to remain on your TV screen for an extended period.

CABLECARD: A card used in HDTVs which allows for Cable TV to be hooked directly into the TV without the need for a Cable TV box. The cablecard will enable the unscrambling of the signal for the know which subscription and premium channels you receive.

CATHODE RAY TUBE: Your ol'' TV picture tube. A cathode ray tube is a vacuum sealed picture tube that uses a cathode ray gun to shoot at the phosphors on the front glass of the tube which creates the picture. See illustrations in HDTV Chapter 2, "How TVs work."

CENTER CHANNEL: Referring to the front speaker in surround sound that is put above or below the TV between the two front speakers. This channel carries the voice or dialogue of the surround sound.

CHANNEL (AUDIO): The sound signal that is sent to a single speaker. In stereo there is a left channel and a right channel; in surround sound it is separated into 6 or 8 channels (5 plus the subwoofer or 7 plus the subwoofer.)

CHANNEL (WHEN REFERRING TO A CHANNEL YOU TUNE INTO): The range of frequencies that bring in a picture signal, like a TV station, or channels on a walkie talkie or portable phone. The device tunes into that range and receives the picture and/or sound information. See Chapter 1 Getting the Picture.

CHROMA: The color information that makes up a color TV picture.

COAX: Short for "coaxial". See below.

COAXIAL AUDIO CABLE: A coaxial cable that carries digital sound. Commonly used between a DVD and a/v receiver or to transfer HDTV digital surround sound. Although it looks like an RCA cable, it carries digital signals for all of the audio channels rather than a single channel like an analog RCA cable. Though some people use an RCA video composite cable, you'll assure your great sound quality by using a coaxial audio cable made to transmit the digital audio.

COAXIAL CABLE: Technically, a coaxial cable can carry different kinds of signals and is a cable that uses a single copper wire to transmit the signal (rather than many twisted wires). While the RF or "F-pin" cable exposes the wire in connecting to a device, other coaxial cables may use RCA connections. The center wire is surrounded by insulation and a braided wire to shield it from interference. (See below for definitions of "RF Cable", "F-pin", and "RCA Connectors.")

COAXIAL DIGITAL CABLE: See "coaxial audio" above.

COMBINED SETUP: This refers to how you route your audio and video in a Home Theater setup. A combined setup sends the video from each of the components to the TV, and the audio from each of the components to the a/v receiver. Some purists insist that this is the best way, but it gets very confusing to use later.

COMPONENT: A piece of audio or video equipment. A device that connects to your TV and/or a/v receiver.

COMPONENT VIDEO: The red, green and blue cables and connections used for DVDs and HDTV. Component video separates each of the red, green and blue signals as well as the luminance (grayscale brightness of colors). This results in a clearer, brighter picture.

COMPOSITE VIDEO: Also called RCA connections. A video signal is made up of chroma (color) and luminance (brightness like grayscale). A composite video cable combines the chroma and luminance into one cable (while an S-Video cable or component video cables separate the signals). (See "Chroma" and "Luminance".)

COMPRESSION: Squeezing large digital information signals to use less storage space or bandwidth. Different kinds of video compression include Mpeg-2 or Mpeg-4. The best kind of compression is "lossless" compression that doesn't lose information to make the signal smaller. (Mpeg 2 and Mpeg 4 are examples of "CoDecs" that are ways to perform COmpression/DECompression)

CONVERGENCE: there are two meanings for convergence. 1. Two different technologies that now work together (like computers and TVs or cell phones and cameras). 2. On Rear Projection TVs, realigning the red, green and blue CRTs so there are distinct lines without red or blue halos. See page

CRT: "Cathode Ray Tube" See above.

D SUB 15: Can refer to the RGB/VGA connection mostly used for computer monitors. See connections chapter 3 "RGB/VGA" connection.

DAC: "Digital to Analog converter." See D/A Converter below and explanation in HDTV chapter 2.

D/A CONVERTER: Digital to Analog Converter. We see and hear in analog light and sound waves, so any signal that has been recorded digitally, must be converted back to analog for us to see and hear. That is the job of a D/A converter. There are different quality converters that can reproduce the original sound and picture more accurately than converters in bargain units.

DCR: "Digital Cable Ready." See below.

DE-INTERLACER: Processes an incoming picture signal to a TV to create a better picture. Can determine if the original material was film or video and make adjustments that clean up artifacts and make the picture clear and clean. This is particularly important when watching a program that was originally shot on film like DVD movies and some TV shows. See HDTV chapter 2. Also see 3:2 pulldown.

DEVICE: A piece of audio or video equipment that creates sound and/or picture which is connected to your TV and/or a/v receiver. Same as "component." May be used in menus or on remotes to mean the same as "source."

DIGITAL AUDIO: Sound that has been created in 1's and 0's like a computer uses and is sent from one device to another via a digital audio cable (see "coaxial audio" or "TosLink"). Digital audio can be encoded for "digital surround sound." (See below.)

DIGITAL CABLE READY: Just like old analog TVs were "cable ready" and you could just hook up the incoming Cable TV's RF cable to your antenna, and change channels; HDTVs are coming equipped with a Digital CableCard that then allows the TV to use its tuner to change channels and hook up directly to the HDTV Digital Cable TV without a cable box. (See "CableCard".)

DIGITAL DECODER: Refers to the digital surround sound decoder found in DVD players and/or a/v receivers. Digital sound may have a variety of formats that must be decoded to hear as it was intended. These formats include Dolby Digital® Surround Sound, Dolby Digital EX®, dts 5.1, Dolby 6.1, DTS-ES™, DVD-Audio, and SACD.

DIGITAL LIGHT PROCESSING™: Can also be referred to as "DLP™". Created by Texas Instruments. Refers to a kind of big screen HDTV that uses a computer chip covered in tiny mirrors which reflect onto the front screen. See HDTV chapter 2 for an explanation of how this TV works.

DIGITAL MICROMIRROR DEVICE: "DMD"; The computer chip used to create the picture in a DLP™ TV.

DIGITAL SOUND: See "digital audio".

DIGITAL SURROUND SOUND: See "AC-3"

DIGITAL VISUAL INTERFACE: "DVI"; see below.

DIGITAL VIDEO RECORDER: "DVR". A device which records from another source, particularly live TV (antenna, Cable TV or Satellite), onto a hard drive similar to a computer. DVRs typically are always recording into a temporary memory which allows you to pause "live TV"

DIPOLAR SPEAKERS: If you want the sound of your back speakers to fill the room, rather than pinpointing the sound coming from behind you or the side, etc., you might be interested in di-polar speakers. Speakers with more than one driver (actual speaker in the cabinet), on opposite sides from one another. The speakers are "out of phase"; they move in opposite directions. This gives an ambient sound, filling the room and gives a sense that you are unable to tell the direction from which the sound is coming, "non-directional." "Electrostatic" and "ribbon" speakers are also considered di-polar because they are "out of phase" and give you the impression that the sound is coming from both back and front.

DIRECT VIEW: The traditional picture tube type TV. Named direct view to refer to the picture created on the front glass in contrast to rear projection. See "CRT".

"DISCRETE" CHANNELS: Refers to audio channels particularly AC-3 digital surround sound. Each channel of sound information that goes to its corresponding speaker (i.e., left front, right surround) has separate and distinct information. This allows for a sense of being surrounded by the action. (For example you hear a door close behind you on your right as it comes from that speaker.)

DLP™ CHIP: The chip created by Texas Instruments used in TVs with "Digital Light Processing" see above.

DMD "Digital Micromirror Display" see above.

DOLBY DIGITAL®: See "AC-3". Dolby Laboratories version of 5.1 surround sound, one of the most popular of the digital surround formats.

DOLBY PRO-LOGIC®: Analog surround sound that delivers 4 channels of sound—left front, right front, center, and rear surrounds. Unlike Dolby Digital where each speaker is "discrete" (see above), the surround speakers reproduce the same sound. Dolby Pro Logic® gets its information from analog stereo inputs where the a/v receiver splits the sound (see "matrixed sound") into the four channels. In this way you can get a type of surround sound from your analog devices like your VCR or MTS stereo TV shows.

DSS/DBS "Digital Satellite System" or "Digital Broadcast Satellite" This is what Satellite TV like DirecTv and Dish network were called when they first were available.

dts: "Digital Theater Systems". A company that creates film and video digital 5.1 surround sound. Competing format of Dolby Digital®, most a/v receivers today have both decoders to accommodate the surround sound of the DVD you are playing.

DTVLink™: Name for iEEE1394 cable — "firewire"— which can carry "5C" copy protection. See HDTV chapter 2, "Copy Protection."

DUAL HOOKUPS OR DUAL CONNECTIONS: When you connect more than one cable to carry the signal from a component to a TV. For example when you

DUAL LNB: What you need to know is that this is a feature that you MUST HAVE on your Satellite dish if you want more than one Satellite receiver and TV on different channels. (See Tuner Chapter 1.) For those who want to know what it is...LNB stands for "low noise block". Your dish receives the signal from the Satellite in the sky. That round white part (called the "feedhorn") picks up the signals reflected off the dish. Each LNB can carry certain channels. When your Satellite receiver asks for a channel (tunes in to a channel), the appropriate LNB sends an amplified signal down the cable to the box. Dual LNB's will have two coaxial outputs from the dish.

DUAL TUNER: Two tuners in one device, each able to tune into separate channels at the same time. Dual Tuner TVs often use the second tuner for Picture in Picture. Satellite and DVRs with dual tuners will record 2 programs at the same time, or record one channel while you watch another.

DVD AUDIO: A high quality sound format for *audio only* version of DVD. Can separate sound, usually music, into digital surround sound (see above). To play DVD Audio you must have a DVD player that plays the format and either the DVD player or (preferably) the a/v receiver must have a DVD Audio decoder (see 6 Channel hookup in Connections chapter 3). The receiver must have 96khz/24 bit (that's the high quality stuff) reproduction capability (some a/v receivers made before 2000 may not be able to play DVD Audio).

DVI: "Digital Visual Interface"; a type of cable and connection that carries video signals. DVI cables can carry digital video signals (as in DVI-D), analog video signals (as in DVI-A), or digital and analog signals (as in DVI-I). The type of DVI cable and DVI connection must match. See connections and cables chapters 3 and 4.

DVR: See "Digital Video Recorder"

ETHERNET: Think "home network". This is the cable or connection that hooks together the computers in your home and now can connect some TVs, DVRs, DVDs and other home theater devices to your home computer so that you can receive movies, photos, music and even the internet through your home theater system. See "convergence" definition at www.home-electronics-survival.com.

FIBER OPTIC CABLES: Cables used to run Cable TV signals (and telephone lines) to your home via a light pulse over a glass optical cable. (Glass is used over long distances, and has a reflective material so the light beams do not interfere with neighboring fiber optic cable beams.)

FIELD: On an interlaced TV, a field is 1/2 of a frame created when the cathode ray gun (CRT) scans across the even lines of pixels (1 field), and then the odd lines of pixels (1 field). This happens at 1/60 th of a second so your eye puts the two images together and perceives a smooth moving picture. One odd and one even field make up a frame. See "FPS", "Frame" and "Interlaced" for more explanation.

FIREWIRE: Name for iEEE1394 coined by Apple Computers. A type of bi-directional digital cable and connection (both input and output in the same cable). Also called iLink™, or DTVLink™. See connections and cable Chapters 2 and 3 for more information.

FIXED PIXEL DISPLAY: TVs like LCD, Plasma or DLP TVs where each pixel receives individual information and appears on the screen at the same time. In contrast a CRT scans lines of pixels intermittently (see "interlaced" or "CRT"). Fixed pixel displays are always "progressive scan". See HDTV Chapter 2 for more information.

F-PIN CABLE (OR F-PIN CONNECTION): An RF cable. The "f-pin" refers to the copper cable that protrudes from the end of the cable and fits into the small hole on the connection terminal. This is the cable used to bring in signal from outside sources like Satellite, Cable TV or an outdoor antenna. See "RF cable" for more information.

FPS: "Frames Per Second" (see below for "Frame"). A moving picture is made up of a number of progressive still photos shown at a fraction of a second. When viewed in succession, the pictures appear to be moving (this is called "persistence of vision"). FPS is a measurement of how many full images of a movie or video is recorded and/or reproduced on the screen in one second. Movies shot on film run at 24 fps; video is recorded at 30 fps. Because a TV set shows 30 frames per second, programs originally shot in film have a better quality when adapted to the 30 fps (see "3:2 pulldown").

FRAME: Each full photo image that makes up a moving picture (see FPS above). On a progressive scan TV each frame is displayed in its entirety. On an "interlaced" TV, each frame is made up of 2 fields. Combining the even line fields and odd line fields is called "interlacing" the picture. "Frame" can also refer to all the picture displayed within the area show on your TV.

FRONT PANEL INPUTS: Jacks or connections found on the front of your TV or device. Commonly used for components that are hooked up temporarily like video game consoles, video cameras etc. May be hidden behind a spring loaded door.

FRONT PROJECTION TV: A TV that uses a projects its image onto a screen similar to the old film projectors. Projection TVs can be connected to a variety of sources like DVD, satellite or cable etc.

FRONT SURROUND SPEAKERS: The left and right speaker that is put to the sides of the TV, in front of you. These speakers carry mostly the front sound affects and music.

HARD DISC RECORDER: (Also called "DVR" or "PVR.") A device that records television programming or other sources onto a hard disc drive similar to that used in your computer. Uses a temporary memory to record a portion of all programming you are currently watching. TiVo and RePlay are types of hard disc recorders.

HD READY: "High Definition Ready". This refers to televisions that can show ATSC but do not have a high definition tuner to receive the stations. HD ready sets need either a set top box, Satellite receiver or cable receiver to tune in to the high definition stations. To be "HD ready" a TV must be able to display a minimum of 720 lines of resolution in progressive scan (720p) and 1080 lines of resolution in interlaced (1080i). See HDTV chapter for more details.

HDCP: High Definition Copy Protection. Encoding on digital media and digital broadcasts that prevents copying a program onto VHS or DVD.

HDMI: "High definition multimedia interface" Used with HDTVs, a cable and connection that carries both digital video and digital audio signals.

HDTV: "High Definition TV". Refers to Televisions with a high definition tuner built in and refers to the whole ATSC digital broadcasts. To be a "true" HDTV, it must be able to display a minimum of 720 lines of resolution in progressive scan (720p) and 1080 lines of resolution in interlaced (1080i). See HDTV chapter for more details.

HI-FI: High Fidelity. Highest quality reproduction of sound. Often used referring to Stereo systems when compared to single channel mono systems (particularly with VCRs; many "hi-fi" VCRs are simply stereo).

HIGH DEFINITION MULTIMEDIA INTERFACE: see "HDMI"

HOME THEATER: The addition of a surround sound system (receiver and speakers) to accompany the picture on a TV. "True" home theater would include a big screen TV but any TV can be part of a home theater. Typically you would listen to the sound from your sound system and watch the video on your TV without sound coming from your TV. (The exception is TVs that create "virtual surround sound" or can connect to speakers and use its internal speaker as the center speaker.) Can also refer to a room created in your home to mimic a theater experience that is specially sound proofed, usually dark, and set up with seats around a big screen TV. See also "surround sound."

HOME THEATER RECEIVER: See A/V receiver.

iEEE1394: A type of bi-directional digital cable and connection (both input and output in the same cable) that started out in the computer world. iEEE1394 was created by the Institute of Electrical and Electronics Engineers ("iEEE"). Also called "firewire", iLink™, or DTVLink™. See connections and cable Chapters 2 and 3 for more information.

iLink™: Sony's name for iEEE1394 or firewire, a bi-directional (both input and output in the same cable), digital connection that carries audio and video or sometimes just audio.

IN-LINE HOOKUP: Connecting an RF cable from the source (antenna, Cable TV or Satellite) into another component (like a VCR or DVR) and then out of the component to the next component (if there is one) and then finally, to the TV.

INPUT: A connection on a device that brings the signal *in* from another source. A cable connects from the output of another device (or from Cable TV or antenna) to the input of a device or the TV.

INTEGRATED TUNERS: A TV or device with the tuner built-in enabling you to change channels on that device. A TV that does not have an integrated tuner is called a "monitor." An HDTV has an integrated tuner; "HD Ready" TVs do not have integrated tuners. VCRs, cable boxes and Satellite receivers are capable of changing channels and therefore could be said to have integrated tuners.

INTERLACED: One way a picture is received and displayed on a TV. Picture tube TVs and some Rear Projection TVs use a CRT which scans the image in even lines and then in odd lines at 1/60th of a second which when these fields are combined, become a complete picture or "frame" (see "FPS" or "frames per second.") Fixed pixel displays like LCD, Plasma and DLP™ do not scan lines and are therefore "**progressive scan**". (See below.)

INTERCONNECTS: Another name for a/v cables; cables that carry audio and/or video signals, gets its name because it connects between two devices.

ISF CERTIFIED-"IMAGING SCIENCE FEDERATION" : A company that sets a high display standard (great picture quality) and trains Home Theater and TV technicians to calibrate your TV to that standard. An ISF DVD is available for brave souls who want to adjust their own TVs. An ISF certified technician, however, will have scopes and tools to do the job more accurately. *Look for this certification if you have a high end installer who is coming in to adjust your system.*

JACK: The connection terminal on a device to which you plug in a cable. They come in different colors and shapes To fit different kinds of cables.

JACK PANEL, "JACK PACK", "INPUT PANEL": On a device you will often find many connections grouped on the back (or side of flat screens). There still may be jacks on the front or other places; the jack panel is where most of the inputs and outputs are found together.

LCD: See "Liquid crystal display"

LCoS: See "Liquid Crystal on Silicon" below.

LIQUID CRYSTAL ON SILICON: A type of TV. This technology is similar to LCD. Because the light is not blocked by the transistor that gives the liquid crystal its information, the picture is brighter than an LCD TV.

LENTICULAR SCREEN: The front screen on rear projection TVs that has tiny ridges which produce a better picture.

LFE: "Low frequency effects". This is the bass of a sound system or the "subwoofer". The deep, booming, rumbling sounds.

LINE AUDIO: An audio cable and connection that carries the audio signal from one channel. For stereo that is right and left cables. For surround sound, there is a separate cable and connection for front right, front left, center, subwoofer, surround right, surround back, etc. 6 or 8 channel line audio is typically used to connect DVD players with DVD Audio (or other surround format) to an a/v receiver not equipped with that decoder.

LINE DOUBLERS : Unlike the name implies, "line doublers" do not *double* the actual scan lines. Instead they typically work by holding the picture for two fields (two 1/2 frames) which creates what appears to be a clearer, brighter picture and eliminates many of the jagged edges that occur during a typical interlaced signal.

LIQUID CRYSTAL DISPLAY: "LCD". A fixed pixel TV (each pixel appears at the same time) that can either display its picture directly (as in a flat panel LCD) or projects its image (as in the larger, LCD projection TV). For an explanation of how this works, see Chapter 2 HDTV.

LUMINANCE: Part of what makes up a color TV picture signal. The "Y" in y/c cables and connections (S-Video). The luminance is the brightness or black and white image that determines shade and hue of the picture. When combined with the Chroma (Color) you see your color TV picture. By keeping the Luminance and chroma separate, there is less processing and the picture remains clearer and brighter.

MAGNETICALLY SHIELDED SPEAKERS: See "**shielded speakers**".

MATRIXED SURROUND SOUND: A code in a stereo signal that then splits the sound into 4 speaker "quadraphonic" (2 front a center and a rear speaker channel.) You can tell matrixed surround because it is hooked up with a right and left audio cable rather than a digital audio connection. See details in Connections Chapter 3 under "RCA Jacks."

Mbps: Mega bits per second. (Also "Mbits/s") A measurement of How many millions of digital bits (individual pieces of information) that can be sent in a second. This relates to TVs in a digital TV broadcast but is more commonly heard when discussing the speed of a DSL or Cable modem internet connection.

MULTICASTING: Broadcasting many channels in the frequencies of a particular TV station. Each ATSC digital channel can carry a wide frequency of information. When not used for the large amount of information of HDTV, a broadcaster can break up the frequencies to send out as many as 5 channels at the same time. Now you can have not only one channel of PBS but a channel for news, for children's shows, etc. See details in HDTV Chapter 2.

NTSC: (National Television Standards Committee). Usually refers to the current analog broadcasts that come to your TV, and that your TV displays (as compared to a new, digital, or HDTV ATSC TV broadcast). When color was added to broadcasts in the 1950's (adopted widely in the 1960s), the NTSC standards ensured that black and white televisions would not become obsolete, continuing to receive signals and display black and white pictures even though they were broadcast in color.

OPTICAL AUDIO: Cables and connections that carry digital sound from DVDs, HDTV or other digital sources. The digital signals travel on a fiber-optic cable as a light beam. Digital audio cables are needed for Digital surround sound like DTS™, Dolby Digital® or DVD audio.

OTA: "Over the Air". Jargon for broadcast signals you receive by antenna.

OUTPUT: Used to describe the audio or video connection on a device from which the signal comes out to be sent to another device for recording or to a TV or home theater receiver to be displayed or heard

PASS-THROUGH: When a device can accept a signal, whether it uses it or not, and passes it through to the next device. A VCR can pass the signal from your antenna, Cable TV or Satellite even when it is not powered on. Many home theater receivers will pass through video signals to a TV. (Other home theater receivers can upgrade or "upconvert" a signal to a better picture quality before sending it out.)

PCM: "Pulse Code Modulation"-- Used to create digital sound. A method for converting analog signals to digital data. You might see this to label a coaxial digital audio connection.

PERSISTENCE OF VISION: Describes why we see movies as moving pictures. The phrase that refers to how our mind processes seeing frames, individual pictures, at a fraction of a second, then strings them together to give the illusion of movement.

PHOSPHORS: What the pixels are made of on a CRT picture tube. The phosphors light up when the electronic beam hits them.

PICTURE-IN-PICTURE: A feature that brings up a little box with a picture on top of the picture screen you are watching. Picture in Picture allows you to watch two channels or sources of programming at the same time (DVD and Cable TV for example.) Often you can move the p.i.p. window around to better see the main picture behind it. A 2 tuner Picture in Picture means the TV can change channels on both pictures but it must be an antenna picture or basic analog cable (or digital cable ready).

P.I.P.: See above "**Picture in Picture**"

PIXEL: Gets its name from "PICture ELement". A group of red, green and blue dots that gets picture information of brightness, hue etc to make up that tiny portion of a picture. Like the grain in a photograph. The mind combines the thousands or millions of pixels to make up the TV picture we see.

PLASMA DISPLAY: A flat panel TV that reproduces video by activating a gas filled chamber that creates the color of a single pixel. Millions of these pixels then make up a single frame of the picture on the display. Plasmas are "fixed pixel displays" (see above). See HDTV chapter 2 for more information about Plasma TVs and details of how they work.

P.O.P: "Picture out of Picture". Like P.I.P, allows the viewer to watch more than one channel or source at the same time. One type of P.O.P. is split screen, another might have more than one screen outside the picture you were watching rather than on top of the other picture being displayed (as in P.I.P.) May be able to change the size of the separate pictures.

PROGRESSIVE SCAN: a way of reading, broadcasting, and displaying pictures where each whole frame is shown at once in contrast to interlaced which divides the frame into fields, showing odd lines of a frame then even lines of a frame. Progressive scan shows 30 whole frames per second; interlaced shows 60 fields per second (with one odd and one even field equalling one frame). Progressive scan gives a smoother, cleaner picture and usually can only be shown on digital TVs or HDTVs.

PROLOGIC® SURROUND SOUND: From Dolby laboratories. See "**Dolby Pro-logic®**"

RADIO WAVES: The analog electromagnetic signal that is broadcast and flows along different "frequencies" to make up the sound and picture that arrives at your TV. The different shapes of the waves create different pictures and sounds. Also see "RF".

RCA COMPOSITE CABLES: The yellow (video), and white and red (audio) cables that carry analog video and audio signals. Called "RCA" because RCA originally developed them. The video cable combines the black and white or "luminance", and the color or "chroma" elements that make up an NTSC picture (In contrast to a Y/C cable that separates the luminance and chroma to create a brighter, more detailed picture).

RCA PHONO PLUG CONNECTORS: Seen on many types of cables from RCA composite and line audio to coax digital sound cables and subwoofer cables. A single tubular shaped end connector that is pushed into your components connection. See illlustrations in Chapter 4, Cables.

REAR SCREEN PROJECTION: A big screen TV that projects an image onto a mirror inside its cabinet, which then reflects the image onto the front screen where you watch the display. Typically rear projection TVs use 3 scanning CRTs. See Chapter 2 HDTV for explanation of how the Rear Projection TV works.

RF: "Radio Frequency" signal. Can refer to the TV broadcast signal that is sent to your antenna. The different TV stations are sent at different frequencies which your tuner brings in when you choose that channel. See Chapter 1 "Getting the Picture."

RF CABLE: This is a coaxial cable characterized by an RF connector with a single, thin, copper cable protruding from the end (see illustrations in Chapter 4- Cables.) It is always used to bring in the signal from Cable TV, a Satellite, or an antenna. It can carry either analog or digital signals. It can also be used to connect between components that use TV signals (like a VCR, DVR, Cable TV or Satellite box) and a TV. RF Cables are used in "**in-line hookups.**"

RF CONNECTION: Also called the "antenna connection." This is the connection on a TV or component that accepts the RF cable (see above.) It is characterized by its screw-on threads and a hole in the center into which the copper cable from the RF connector fits. A TV will always have at least an RF connection (unless it is older than the early 1980's). A DVD and a home theater receiver will almost *never* have an RF connection.

RF MODULATOR: An accessory used when you only have an RF connection on your TV and your component uses only an RCA composite connection. The RCA composite cables are connected to the RF modulator which then connects to the TV with an RF cable via the RF (or "antenna") connection. The RF modulator also changes the RCA composite incoming signal so that it can be received on channel 3 (or 4) of your TV.

RF REMOTE CONTROL: A remote control that uses an RF signal ("radio frequency signal" —see below.) to send the instructions to the TV or component. Where a typical, infrared remote control must be "seen" by the component you are trying to control, an RF remote control can be used from anywhere within the signal's range without "line of sight." This means you can change the channel or turn up the sound on a device that is behind the doors of a cabinet or control a device that is in the living while you are in another room like the kitchen or bathroom.

RF SIGNAL: "Radio frequency signal" sends information, a remote control command, an audio signal to wireless headphones, etc., through sound waves that are received by an antenna. Typically these signals are not strong and can only travel limited distances (you probably couldn't change the channel on a TV at the neighbor's house).

RG-6 CABLE: This refers to coaxial cable used to carry digital transmissions such as digital Satellite or Cable TV. Earlier cables used in analog Cable TV were RG-5.9. (These ratings go back to World War II and have little meaning to most of us laymen other than to know you want RG-6 for digital signals including bringing in HDTV.)

RGB: Stands for "Red, Green Blue" which are the colors of the pixels on your TV and the color of the CRTs. The primary colors when painting are red, yellow, and blue and all other colors can be created from them. In light, the primary colors that make up all other colors is red, green and blue. Component video connections will be red, green and blue as the picture is separated into the individual color elements (See "component video for a clear explanation.)

RGB-HV: Stands for Red, Green, Blue, Horizontal, Vertical. This is a connection used in High Definition TV, often connecting a set top high definition tuner to a TV. The Horizontal and Vertical is a sync pulse needed on components that use this connection. (See Chapters 3 & 4, Connections and Cables.)

RPTV: Rear Projection TV. See "**Rear Screen Projection TV**"

RS-232: A digital serial connection like that found on your computer. When found on a home theater component like a DVR or a/v receiver, it is often used for one device to control the other. For example a DVR might connect to a Satellite or Cable TV box so that it can change its channel when you change the channel on the DVR.

SACD: "Super Audio CD". An audio format used by Sony which created 5.1 channel sound used for music. A DVD player with an SACD decoder could play these CDs for high quality, digital surround sound music. Similar to DVD-Audio. SACD has been discontinued, but equipped DVD players still can play SACD in all its glory.

SET TOP BOX: Often refers to a separate tuner, particularly used for HDTV, that receives and changes the channel for a TV that does not have an "integrated tuner." May also refer to a Cable TV box which includes a tuner to change channels.

SHIELDED SPEAKERS: Speakers designed to protect other equipment from the effects of the speakers' magnets. Speakers use large magnets to reproduce sound. Magnets can interfere with televisions, computer monitors and computers causing color distortions and other problems. You will want to be sure any speaker placed next to a TV or computer is shielded (particularly a center speaker placed on top of a TV.)

SIGNAL: The audio and/or video information that flows in and out of your components which ultimately you see on your TV and hear from speakers (either speakers on the TV or separate home theater speakers.) The quality of the signal is altered by the quality of the connections on the component and the quality of the cable.

SIMULCAST: Broadcast in more than one way at the same time. There is various audio simulcasts where you can tune into a different sound channel to hear another language or for the sight impaired. Simulcast is commonly used today to refer to a TV station that is broadcasting a program both in analog traditional NTSC at the same time they are sending out the signal in High Definition.

SOURCE: Refers to the source of the audio and video you want to watch. Where the signal is coming from, whether it is broadcast TV, via antenna, Satellite or Cable TV; or it is another source like a DVD player playing a DVD, a DVR playing a show it has recorded, or a VCR playing a VHS tape.

SOURCE SELECTOR: This is a term used in Chapter 5, Preparation and Hookup which refers to how you will choose what you will watch and listen to on your home theater. You can choose to change between sources (change inputs) through your TV or through your home theater a/v receiver or a combination.

SPLIT PIN RCA CONNECTOR: A cable connector end improvement which results in better transfer of signal. An "RCA connector" where the pin is separated rather than solid, allowing for more surface connection between the cable end and the connector on the device.

SPLIT SCREEN: 2 pictures on the screen, usually side-by-side. Split screen works like Picture in Picture but the pictures are next to each other rather than on top of each other. Some split screen TVs have a feature where you can resize one frame to be larger or smaller than the other.

SPLITTERS: An accessory that allows you to take in the signal from one RF cable and split it off into two outputs. Often used to split an analog Cable TV signal, or can be used to split a signal coming out of a cable or Satellite box where you will watch the same show on more then one TV.

STEREO: Audio that comes out of two speakers, a right and a left channel. "Stereo" might be used to refer to an audio receiver with speakers (and might even be referred to as a "stereo" even if it has surround sound.)

SUBWOOFER: The speaker that plays the low frequency sounds or "bass" in a 5.1 surround sound system (it is the .1). The subwoofer gives the sense of rumbling in a movie soundtrack.

SUPER VHS VCR: A VCR with a better quality picture that has up to 425 lines of resolution in comparison with regular VHS that has 330 maximum lines of resolution. You need to use Super VHS tapes to get the quality unless your machine has a feature to record super vhs onto regular tapes.

SURGE: A flood of power that comes through the electric power line, that can damage equipment by bringing in more power than the equipment's components can handle. A surge often follows a power outage as the current races back into your home. See explanation under "Surge Protectors" in the "Accessories" section of the Hookup Prep and Planning Chapter 5.

SURGE PROTECTOR: An accessory that looks like a power strip but has the ability to stop a surge of power from being flooded through the electrical power cords into your devices. Some surge protectors also protect from power surges that may come through outside RF cable sources (antenna, Satellite or Cable TV) or that may come through telephone lines. See "surge" above. See explanation under "Surge Protectors" in the "Accessories" section of the Hookup Prep and Planning Chapter 5.

SURROUND SPEAKERS: Refers to the back speakers in a surround sound or 5.1 digital surround sound set up.

SURROUND BACK SPEAKERS: Refers to a speaker or speakers that are used in extended digital surround like 6.1 surround or 7.1 surround used in DTS-ES™ or Dolby Digital EX®

SURROUND SOUND: Home Theater sound where speakers are set up to surround you with sound. Surround Sound includes analog surround sound like Dolby ProLogic® or DTS Neo:6™ and it refers to digital surround sound like Dolby Digital® or dts 5.1.

SVGA, XVGA: Refers to the resolution of a VGA, computer monitor. XVGA has a higher resolution, close to that of high definition.

S-VIDEO: A cable and connection that carries a video signal separating the black and white, and the color information that make up an analog video signal. See "y/c cable" for more details.

TERMINAL: The input or output connection on your component, TV, or a/v receiver, into which the end of a cable connects. Also called "jacks", "inputs", "outputs", "connections."

THX: THX is an audio certification created when George Lucas visited movie theaters to assure the sound of the movie "STAR WARS" was reproduced at the quality Lucas had intended. Standards were later created for home theater, and other consumer devices that create sound. THX certified equipment assures you that the equipment, and all of the speakers will sound good together, will "match". Look for THX Select is for smaller rooms under 2000 square feet.

TIME SHIFTING: Recording a TV program so that you can watch it at a time that is convenient for you.

TosLink: A digital sound cable and connection that sends sound by light travelling over an optical cable (sometimes called Optical digital sound). Toslink uses a plastic optical fiber to run the light rather than glass. Gets its name "TosLink" because it is was invented by the manufacturer, "Toshiba." See Chapters 3 & 4 about connections and cables for more information.

TRANSMISSIVE: A type of projection TV. A transmissive projection TV shines light through a small panel (like an LCD or LCoS chip) directly onto the screen, in contrast to a rear projection TV projects its image onto a mirror that reflect onto the screen you watch. See HDTV chapter 3 for illustrations and more explanation.

UHF BAND: Ultra High Frequency. Channels that are sent over the frequencies above channel 13. See Tuner chapter 1 to learn more about channels, frequencies and bands.

UPCONVERSION: Taking a lower quality signal and processing it to send or show in higher quality or resolution. Used in high definition TV to refer to a signal that is sent at a lower resolution, but is then processed to increase the resolution to be shown on HDTV. This is often done when watching an HDTV where NTSC picture resolution shows a grainy picture. Upconversion can show a better quality picture than would otherwise be seen. There are a number of ways to upconvert including "line doubling" and "scaling". See HDTV chapter 2 for more on upconversion.

UPCONVERT: Taking a lower quality signal and processing it to resemble a better signal. As in upconversion this can happen in picture quality. Upconverting can also describe how an a/v receiver can accept a signal from an RCA composite cable and convert it to be output through an S-Video cable or component video cable (it also upconverts S-Video to component video.)

USB: "Universal Serial Bus". A type of connection typically used to connect computers to various devices like keyboards, your mouse, external drives. Can be used in TV systems to connect a device to a wireless receiver or network card so that it can receive information from your computer.

VGA: Usually refers to a computer monitor display. Another label for the RGB connection.

VHF BAND: The range of TV broadcast frequencies that carry TV channels from channel 2 to channel 13. See Tuner Chapter 1 for more information on frequencies, bands, and channels.

VIDEO SELECTOR: An accessory into which you can plug several devices with one output to connect to the TV. This accessory is used when you have more components with RCA , S-video, or component connections than you have available inputs on your TV. Once you plug your components into the accessory, you can push a button (convenient when they come with a remote control) to change which device you want to watch.

VIEWING ANGLE: Measured in degrees, this tells you how far to the side of the TV you can view a TV and still get a good picture. Some kinds of TVs will look distorted or fade in contrast when viewed far to the side.

WI-FI: Slang term for wireless technology.

WIRELESS: A signal sent from one device to another without connecting actual cables between them. The signal is sent via a transmitter (like a router) to an access point or a wireless network card. Also used to refer to a device or accessory that is typically connected by cables (i.e. wireless headphones or wireless speakers). See "Wireless" section of Cables Chapter 3.

Y/C (CABLE): Also called "**S-Video**". This cable separates the "Y" or grayscaled black and white picture information called "luminance" (because it determines the brightness and hue of the colors), from the "C" or color called "chroma" which carries the information of what color each pixel will be to make up the complete picture. This separation creates a sharper, brighter picture quality because it sends the signal the way the TV station sends it and the way a traditional TV displays it.

Appendix

USEFUL WEBSITES
MORE IN DEPTH INFORMATION
ONLINE MAGAZINES
CONSUMER INFORMATION
ONLINE SHOPPING ASSISTANCE
ONLINE ELECTRONICS STORES
MANUFACTURER'S INFORMATION

WEBSITES

The web has a number of resources to help you choose, set up, and use your equipment. You can get detailed explanations to increase your understanding on a a number of topics. You can find user's manuals for your equipment. (Alas, you don't have to worry where you placed your manual!) There are magazines to keep you up-to-date. And, of course, you can shop online. It can get overwelming to sift through all the information without a place to start. So, here are some websites I have found to be easy to understand to get you started. This list is by no means complete.

For updated information, new gadgets and features, advice, troubleshooting, definitions and more:

www.home-electronics-survival.com

(Be sure to sign up for our newsletter to have the newest information as technology changes several times per year.)

Technology Explained
Details of how technology works in (somewhat) simple terms.

> www.hometheater.about.com or www.homeelctronic.about.com
> **www.howstuffworks.com** *Fun site. Go to electronics or type in what you want to learn more about (i.e., LCD TV, home theater, HDTV, etc. You can also learn how fire breathing works while you are there!)*

Magazines Online
Learn what's new, reviews of products, more how-to aricles.

> www.hometheatermag.com *Relatively easy to understand, lots of reviews.*
> www.cnet.com
> www.soundandvisionmag.com
> www.widescreenreview.com *If you want to know about high end home theater.*
> www.electronicHouse.com *For those who like TVs in every room....*
> www.hemagazine.com *Another high end home theater guide*
> www.dtvmag.com *Digital verrsion of Curtco's Digital TV magazine. Good basics on Digital and HDTV. What's new and reviews.*
> www.ceLifestyles.com *This magazine covers all aspects of gadgets from MP3 players to wireless telephones. It also has a lot of informtion about home theater, written on what I would consider to be above beginner level.*

Organizations:

www.ce.org **Consumer Electronics Association.** *This is the group to which all major manufacturers and retailers belong. CE lobbies for technologies, is a big player in making HDTV happen, and is involved in retailer and consumer education. They also put on CES, the international consumer electonics show each January that sets the pace of things to come for the following year.*

www.cedia.net **Custom Electronic Design and Installation Association**. *Members can take courses and receive certification. If you are looking for an installer and don't have anyone who can refer one, this is the place to go.*

www.dtv.gov *Can keep you updated on what's coming in Digital TV and programming today.*

www.checkhd.com *Might be able to tell you what HD you can receive in your area. You can click on "over the air antenna" or "satellite/cable".*

Consumer Information

www.consumerreports.com
www.consumerfay.com *Great advice about electronics and more.*

Online Buying Advice

www.consumersearch.com (Go to the area marked "Electronics Reviews" or click directly on the component you want.) *This is a great site. It encapsulates many reviews and gives you a summary to follow. Once it has helped you with advice it connects you to a comparison of prices and sites where you can buy the component.*

www.crutchfieldadvisor.com
www.epinions.com
www.plasmatvbuyingguide.com
www.beststuff.com

Online Price Comparisons

Using comparison sites, you can find the best price for the model you like. You also can find other consumer's opinions of the product as well as the online website's customer service and reliability.

www.shopzilla.com *This is the shopping search for bizrate.com. It will give you all prices, reviews and retailer sites reliability.*

www.pricegrabber.com
www.shopping.com
www.google.com (Click on "froogle" for shopping searches.)

Online Retailers

(Many online retailers have a glossary of terms and features explained as well as buying advice so look around for "resources", "buying guides" or any "glossary". Also note that when words or features are underlined, you might be able to click on them to learn more or see the term defined.

www.circuitcity.com
www.bestbuy.com (the research center is great!)
www.crutchfields.com
www.tweeter.com
www.thegoodguys.com
www.radioshack.com (ACCESSORIES)
www.onecall.com
www.amazon.com
www.techdepot.com
www.buy.com
www.sears.com
www.target.com
www.overstock.com
www.audioadvisor.com

Manufacturers

You might want to check out the manufacturers websites to learn more about their products, what their jargon and features are, and some offer direct sales. Manufacturers websites are helpful in the "support" area where you can type in your model # and get answers to frequently asked questions or troubleshoot a problem. Also, most sites now offer owner's manuals to download (in case you've missplaced the one you didn't read when you got your equipment).

Some manufacturers websites offer tutorials of how to use the menus or explanations of technology and how things work.

www.usa.denon.com for Home Theater
www.definitivetech.com (speakers)
www.hitachi.us   (And you'll have to make your way to "home" and "Video")
www.jvc.america.com
www.mitsubishi--tv.com
www.monstercable.com Go to the interactive hook up guide for help with connecting your equipment or to "Hookup & Learning."
www.onkyousa.com
www.panasonic.com (click on consumer electronics)
www.philipsusa.com (There's a great tutorial on HDTV.)
www.pioneerelectronics.com
www.rcaaudiovideo.com
www.samsung.com (Click on "products" and then click on "TV, Video & Audio.") You can also go to www.samsung.com/dtvguide/ for an excellent tutorial about how TVs and DTV works.

www.sharpusa.com   (Go to "entertainment" and pick your interest. On the "televisions page you can get a comparison of LCD vs. Plasma, and other information.)

www.sonystyle.com (click on TV & Video) Then look around for "sony 101" where there are great tutorials for you to learn more about how to use your Sony product.

www.tacp.toshiba.com (Go to "What to Look For" to learn more about the Toshiba products, features, terms, and technology).

www.tivo.com

www.yamaha.com for Home Theater.

Satellite and Cable Providers:

www.directv.com

www.dishnetwork.com

http://www.ncta.com/industry_overview/top50mso.cfm **National Cable & Telecommunictions Association.** (This is the page that links to the top 50 cable TV providers in the U.S. Click on the cable provider name and then click on theURL (link) on the company's information page.)

www.comcast.com

www.adelphia.com

Useful Resources:

www.antennaweb.org (learn what kind of antenna you need at your address to receive the greatest number of channels. NEEDED FOR OVER-THE-AIR HDTV!)

www.remotes.com

www.imagingscience.com (To find ISF certified tech to tune up the picture on your TV.)

www.dolby.com Details about surround sound and room setup.

www.dts.com/consumer Details on creating dts environment, DVD and D-VHS titles listed.

MAGAZINES

(A partial list, note online magazines for their print counterparts.)

Home Theater Magazine
CeLifestyles
Digital TV
CE Tips
Sound and Vision
E-Gear
Widescreen Review

International TV Broadcast Standards
PAL & SECAM

See HDTV Chapter 2 for information about different TV broadcast and display systems.   Here is a list of countries and which system they use. This will be helpful if you were to purchase equipment overseas or a DVD or VHS tape.

Countries that use
SECAM

(Sequential Couleur Avec Memoire or Sequenial Color with Memory)

Armenia	East Germany	Ivory Coast	Monaco	Togo
Azerbaijan	Egypt	Latvia	Mongolia	Tunisia
Belarus	Estonia	Lebanon	Morocco	Ukraine
Benin	France	Libya	New Caledonia	Zaire
Bosnia	French Guyana	Liechtenstein	Niger	
Bulgaria	Gabon	Lithuania	Russia	
Burundi	Greece	Luxemburg	Saint Pierre	*MESECAM
Chad	Guadeloupe	Madagascar	Saudi Arabia *	
Congo	Guyana Republic	Mali	Senegal	
Croatia	Hungary	Martinique	Slovenia	
Czechoslovakia	Iran	Mauritania	Syria	
Dijibouri	Iraq	Mauritius	Tahiti	

Countries that use
PAL (Phase Alternating Line)

Afghanistan	Ghana	North Korea	Uganda
Albania	Gibraltar	Norway	UnitedArab Emir-
Algeria	Greenland	Oman	ates
Angola	Guinea	Pakistan	United Kingdom
Argentina **	Holland Hong	Paraguay **	Uruguay **
Australia	Kong Iceland	Poland	West Germany
Austria	India Indonesia	Portugal	Yemen
Azores	Ireland	Qutar	Yugoslavia
Baharain	Israel	Romania	Zambia
Bangladesh	Italy	S.W. Africa	Zimbabwe
Belgium Botswana	Jordan	Singapore	* = PAL- M
Brazil *	Kenya	Somalia	* * = PAL- N
Brunei	Kuwait	South Africa	
Cameroon	Laos	Spain	
Canary Islands	Liberia	Sri Lanka	
Cyprus	Madeire Malaysia	Sudan	
Denmark	Malta	Swaziland	
Dubai	Mozambique	Sweden	
England	Nepal	Switzerland	
Ethiopia	New Guinea	Tanzania	
Faeroe Islands	New Zealand	Thailand	
Finland	Nigeria	Turkey	

Countries that use
NTSC (National Television Standards Committee)

Antigua	Ecuador	Philippines
Bahamas	El Salvador	Puerto Rico
Barbados	Guam	Saint Kitts
Barbuda	Guatemala	Saint Lucia
Belize	Haiti	Saint Vincent
Bermuda	Honduras	Saipan
Bolivia	Jamaica	Samoa
Burma	Japan	South Korea
Cambodia	Mexico	Surinam
Canada	Midway Islands	Taiwan
Cayman Islands	Netherland Antilles	Tobago
Chile	Nicaragua	Trinidad
Colombia	North Mariana Island	United States
Costa Rica	Panama	Venezuela
Cuba	Peru	Virgin Islands

The following chart gives you a look at the technical difference between the different systems/standards. Mostly, the chart shows you, in numbers, why one system won't play on another. It is interesting to note the number of displayable lines of resolution (higher number=better picture).

SYSTEM:	SECAM B,G,H	SECAM D,K,K1,L	PAL	PAL N	PAL M	NTSC	ATSC
# OF LINES/ DISPLAYABLE- LINES/ # OF FIELD	625/576 /50	625/576 /50	625/576 /50	625/576 /50	525/480 /60	525/480 /60	480 SDTV 720 or 1080 HDTV/ 60 fields interlaced or 30 fields progressive
HORIZONTAL FREQUENCY	15.625 kHZ	15.625 kHZ	15.625 kHZ	15.625 kHZ	15.750 kHZ	15.734 kHZ	
VERTICAL FREQUENCY	50 Hz	50 Hz	50 Hz	50 Hz	60 Hz	60 Hz	50 Hz
VIDEO BANDWIDTH	5.0 MHz	5.0 MHz	5.0 MHz	4.2 MHz	4.2 MHz	4.2 MHz	n/a

Although this chart includes ATSC, there is really no comparison as it is not actually sent in a width of frequencies like analog television.

3:2 (OR 2:3) PULLDOWN EXPLAINED

As noted in the HDTV Chapter 2, with de-interlacers and 3:2 pulldown, an equipped TV can correct for loss of picture quality. It is particularly important for programs that were originally film (versus video), like DVDs, movies and some TV shows. The original 24 frames per second must be matched to the 30 frames per second of video through a process called **3:2 PULLDOWN** (or sometimes 2:3 pulldown). The reason for the name change is that the sequence was originally 3 fields then 2 fields but has changed as deinterlacers changed (see below).

To turn 24 frames of film into 60 interlaced fields (or 30 frames per second for video), the deinterlacer grabs 2 video fields from the first film frame.

Then it takes 3 fields from the next film frame.

It repeats in this 2 field/3 field sequence.

When it's done, 2 film frames = 5 video fields which take the same amount of time to display— .08 seconds.

Index

D

H

hard disc recorder 40, 88,205. *See* DVR
HD15 101, 103
HDCP 46, 56, 86, 100, 101, 131, 206
HDD (hard disc recorder) *See* DVR
HDMI 56, 86, 87, 89, 100, 101, 102, 111, 112, 120, 125, 130, 132, 134, 135, 206
HDTV VI, 13, 15, 16, 19, 24, 28, 30, 34, 43, 52, 53, **55-84**, **97-101**, 106, 107, 111, 113, **129-134, 176**,
HDTV Format 64
HD ready 30, 66, 67, 84, 103, 156, 201, 205
HI-FI 63, 86, 206
high definition *See* HDTV
High Definition TV *See* HDTV
Home Theater 18, 43, 51, 81, 106, 107, 108, 116, 137, 138, 148, 154, 166
Home theater in a Box 43
HOOKUP WORKSHEET 151, 153
horizontal resolution 63
HTiB   43 *See* Home theater in a Box

I

iEEE1394 X, XI, 56, 102, 107, 125, 134, 135, 136, 139, 140, 204, 205, 206
iLink 56, 102, 125, 134, 139
in-line hookup 38, 156, 162, 209
input 34, 36, 37, 39, 43, 88, 91, 92, 93, 94, 98, 99, 101, 102, 108, 111, 112, 116, 117, 121, 123, 126, 128, 134, 138, 139, 151, 152, 155, 156, 157, 159, 160, 162, 163, 164, 182, 183, 189, 190, 191, 194, 195, 196, 200, 201, 205, 206, 211
INPUT jack 87
Interconnects 121,141
interlaced 60, 61, 64, 66, 69, 78, 205, 207, 208, 214, 215
internet 44, 48, 51, 56, 57, 142, 143, 204, 207
ISF Certified 47, 71, 206, 221

J

jacks 44, 87, 88, 89, 91, 92, 96, 98, 105, 107, 108, 110, 111, 113, 116, 117, 148, 149, 152, 155, 160, 172, 183, 207, 211. *See also* terminals, connections
jack pack 110
jaggies 55

Over-the-Air Antenna 83
over the air 52, 219. *See also* off air, OTA, broadcast
oxygen-free cables 122

P

P.I.P. 22, 34, 208. *See* Picture in Picture
P.O.P. (Picture Out of Picture) 34 *See also* Split Screen
PAL TV system 50, 213, 214
pass-through signal 38, 94, 95, 114, 160, 163, 183
PCM 86, 107, 120, 208
Persistence of Vision 60, 205
Picture in Picture **34**, 146, 204, 208, 211
pixel 61, 72, 73, 74, 75, 76, 78, 205, 206, 207, 208, 212
Placement of equipment 161, 173, 174
Plasma TV 44, 61, 64, 65, 68, 71, 73, **75**, 78, 103, 176, 201, 205, 206, 208
Powell Plan 55, 58
power conditioner 185, 186, 197
premium cable or satellite channel 18, 24, 26, 28, 29, 34, 42, 56, 67, 82, 84, 88, 201
progressive scan **61**, 62, 64, 65, 66, 69, 72, 96, 98, 129, 205, 206, 208
projection TV   69, 70, 72, 73, 76, 77, 207, 212 *See also* Front projector
PVR. *See* DVR

Q

quadraphonic 79, 207

R

radio frequency 25, 35, 36, 48, 62, 91, 126, 131, 143, 200, 209 *See also* RF.
radio wave 48
RCA 24, 43, 52, 63, 72, 73, 79, 86, 89, 92, 93, 94, 96, 99, 105, 107, 108, 115, 116, 117, 120, 124,
        127, 128, 129, 132, 136, 137, 138, 140, 151, 157, 160, 161, 182, 183, 194, 201, 202, 209,
        210, 212
RCA cable 107, 128, 137, 161, 202
RCA jack 92, 160
REAR PROJECTION 44, 69
remote control 35, 37, 88, 156, 157, 182, 183, 209, 212
resolution 13, 62, 63, 65, 66, 75, 124, 126, 127, 128, 130, 131, 175, 183, 211, 212, 214
RF, 22, 25, 27, 35, 36, 38, 62, 63, 86, 87, 91, 94, 114, 120, 124, 126, 127, 135, 143, 146, 151,
        156, 157, 158, 160, 174, 183, 189, 194, 197, 200, 202, 203, 205, 206, 209, 211
        See also radio frequency.
RF modulator 156, 183, 209
RF remote control 174

RF signal 25, **36**
RGB 86, 96, 99, 103, 120, 125, 129, 132, 133, 202, 210
RGB-HV 86, 96, 99, 103, 125, 132, 210
RG 6 cable 27
RJ-45 109
RPTV 47, **69**, 70, 72, 75, 210. *See also* REAR PROJECTION
RS-232 109, 210.

S

S-VHS 94, 95, 114, 160
S-Video 38, **94-95**, 96, 114, 122, 124, **128**, 157, **160**, 161, 165, 182, 186, 191, 202, 207, 211, 212
SACD 42, 81, 105, 117, 139, 140
Satellite 15, 17, **18**, 23, 24, 25, **27,** 28, 29, **30**, 31, **32-35**, 36, 37, 38, 40, 41, 43, 57, 58, 67, 81, 82, **84**, 87, 88, 91, 94, 95, 106, 107, 109, 114, 121, 124, 126, 127, 128, 129, 138, 154, 156, 157, 158, 160, 162, 164, 166, 173, 183, 189, 193, 194, 195, 196, 197, 203, 204, 205, 206, 208, 209, 210, 21
Satellite dish 25, **27**, 28, 34, 82, 84, 126, 204
scaler 55
scrambled picture (signal) 18, 28, 29, 55, 154
SDTV 65, 66, 214
SECAM TV system 50, 213
set top box 18, 28, 30, 32, 34, 64, 67, 99, 132
shielded cable 122,
shielded speaker 177, 178, 210
simulcast 52, 58
Source Selector   148, 155
spade connector 141
speakers 17, 18, 43, **79-81** , 93, 105, 113, 116, 118, **141**, 143, 148, 150, 156, 157, **169**, **177-181**, **187, 188, 192, 193**, 195, 196, 201, 203, 204, 205, 206, 207, 210, 211, 220
split V, VI, 34, 35, 79, 183, 207
splitter 183
split pin 120, 210
split screen 34
spring loaded speaker connection141, 205
stereo 17, 18, 43, 63, 79, 80, 91, 92, 93, 96, 105, 108, 126, 127, 135, 136, 156, 162, 200, 201, 204, 206, 207, 211
streaming video 44
subwoofer 79, 108, 118, 140, 177, 200, 201, 207, 209, 211
surge protector 184, 185, 211
surround sound 13, 15, 18, 42, 43, 46, 51, 63, 65, **79,** 80, 81, 92, 93, 105, 106, 107, 108, 112, 117, 126, 128, 135, 136, 137, 140, 150, 155, 156, 157, 158, 160, 167, 174, 177, 178, 179, 181, 195, *See also* 5.1 channel surround, digital surround, Dolby Digital®, DTS

T

terminal 91, 93, 94, 99, 102, 113, 201, 205, 207
THX 146, **177**, 211
timeshift 55
TiVo 19, 205
TosLink 86, 106, 117, 120, 136, 137, 138, 191, 203, 212
Transition to HDTV **58**
TRANSMISSIVE **70**, 212
tuner 18, 19, 29, 30, 31, 32, 33, 34, 35, 36, 37, 38, 39, 43, 52, 65, 67, 82, 84, 97, 99, 130, 131, 132,
     183
turbine 123
TV-Based 156, 194

U

UHF 19, 22, **24**, 31, 35, 48, 52, 82, 83, 113, 201, 212
upconversion 157, 158, **161**, 212
UPCONVERT 47, 64, 212

V

VCR 14, 18, 33, 34, 37, 38, **40**, 41, 43, 55, 63, 64, 87, 88, 114, 117, 121, 126, 151, 154, 159, 160,
     162, 164, 182, 183, 197
VHF 19, **24**, 31, 113
Video Selector 182
viewing angle 75, 76, 78, 167, 174
viewing distance 175
VTR 38

W

WEB TV 34, **44** ,127
Wi-fi 120, 142, 212
wireless 24, 57, 109, 142, 143, 179, 200, 209, 212, 218

X

Y

Y/C 86, 94, 120, 128, 209, 212
Y/C cable 120, 128, 209
y/c cable 120, 128, 209

Z

Now that you have become comfortable with your TV & Home Electronics...

...You probably know others who could benefit.

To order copies of

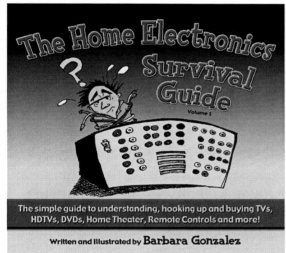

The Home Electronics Survival Guide

go to:
www.easier.tv
and click on "Buy Now"

or send a check or money order
for $24.95 to
**Home Electronics Survival
P.O. Box 1296
Cedar Ridge, CA 95924**

Home Electronics Survival.com

Get simple-to-understand information on our website!

www.easier.tv or
www.home-electronics-survival.com

Sign up for our NEWSLETTER for updates and special offers and new products to make your life simple.

INFORMATION is frequently added to the website to help you understand the newest gadgets, features and technology news.

Order e-books: *"STOP THE OVERWHELM! Shopping for Electronics"*
         and   *"Let THEM do it— How to find and work with an Installer"*

Listen to what's new on Internet Radio! Listen or call in with questions about new gadgets, innovations and technologies in a way YOU can really understand!

Keep your eyes open for:

"How to Make More Money by Having More Fun—A Guide to Selling Electronics and More"

The Home Electronics Survival Guide Volume 2
— Setting up and Using your TV, Home Theater, Remote Controls and more..."